CALAVERAS COUNTY ILLUSTRATED

Calaveras County

Illustrated

And Described

SHOWING ITS

ADVANTAGES

FOR HOMES.

LITHOGRAPHED AND PUBLISHED BY

W. W. ELLIOTT & CO.,

921 BROADWAY, OAKLAND, CAL.

1885.

FACSIMILE REPRODUCTION - 1991 - LINROSE PUBLISHING - FRESNO, CALIFORNIA

PREFACE

In a period of twenty years, 1873 to 1893, more than fifty books were published dealing with either the history or current activities of Northern California counties or regions. Both types of books supplied a wealth of information that would otherwise have been lost. This book is one of the latter type, an illustrated account of the people, attractions and beauties of nature in one of the largest —and most representative—counties in the Mother Lode area of 1885.

Foremost among the publishers of such books was Wallace W. Elliott of Oakland and San Francisco. In addition to this book he produced twenty-two others by himself and six more in partnership with either Clarence L. Smith or E. S. Moore.

This book has been reproduced to be as much like the original as possible, at the same time using modern production facilities for economy and quality. For those who note the absence of pages 83, 84, 95, 96, 101 and 102, we can only report that they were not in the original book. This was confirmed by reference to four different copies of the original edition.

The absence of these pages is probably the result of cancellation of space by supporters. This type of book was, in the final analysis, made possible by the support of local people who were willing to buy space for a portrait, a family picture or an engraving of their ranch or residence. This practice led to these books' being called mug books—people wanted to see their "mugs" in print. We should be happy that they did. They—and others—ordered the books in advance of publication, so the books were also called by the more dignified name of "subscription editions."

The field sketch of Sheep Ranch City on pages 108 and 109 indicates that that small community planned a cooperative participation in the book but cancelled it before publication. Too bad.

We are indebted to Mrs. Claire Soracco of Angels Camp and to her grandfather, Joseph Oneto, who subscribed for the original book which Mrs. Soracco loaned for reproduction in 1976.

The popularity of local histories was sparked by a wave of patriotism, pride and interest in our history created by the celebration of the United States Centennial in 1876. About 80 percent of these history books were published between 1876 and 1885. Only a few more were published between 1885 and the mid-1890s when the country was wracked by a severe depression.

The first reprint of this book, in 1976, was a project of the Calaveras County Bicentennial Commission. The 1991 reprint is appropriately supported by the Calaveras County Historical Society. Its members, along with Linrose Publishing Company of Fresno, are to be congratulated for making available again this valuable portrayal of life more than 100 years ago in Calaveras County and California's Mother Lode country.

Charles W. Clough, historian
1991

EXPLANATORY.

THIS work is in no sense a history. The aim has been by a selection of descriptive articles and a variety of illustrations to show the resources of Calaveras County, its natural scenery, and thus attract people to its many advantages for homes. Articles were selected from a great variety of competent sources of information. The description of prominent farms and homes, in connection with the views of them, will give a stranger a better idea of situation than could be done by any other means.

The publishers, W. W. Elliott & Co., lithographers, Oakland, Cal., make a specialty of getting up illustrated descriptive works, keeping artists and engravers adapted to this line of work constantly employed.

CALAVERAS COUNTY,
CALIFORNIA.

CALAVERAS County, to which a large proportion of the miners in halcyon days of "'49 and '50" betook themselves and from whose hills and gulches million upon million of gold have been poured into the treasury of the world, has an area of 622,000 acres. Here are found some of the best mines in this State, and the entire county may, in fact, be regarded as a bed of mineral deposits. The baser metals, copper, iron, cinnabar, etc., are found in abundance, and ledges of marble, limestone, and granite, and undeveloped deposits of coal are known to exist.

Calaveras is now attracting attention as a fruit and vineyard country, and its foot-hills are being occupied and covered with fruit trees and vines that are yielding good returns and promise well for the future.

Calaveras is a wonder land, having more general and especial natural curiosities than any other county in the State. Among these we may mention the Big Trees, Natural Bridges, Hot Springs, Extensive Caves, Basaltic Cliffs, Table Mountain, and others world-wide in reputation.

If a person would travel over the county he would find a never ending panorama of grand and pleasant scenes; the old abandoned mining grounds and towns going to decay; the present successful quartz and copper mines; extensive mining ditches bringing water long distances over hill and valley to supply the miner and the farmer; this canal winding its sinuous way on the top or around the sides of the ridge, or its sparkling contents rushing impetuously down the water-furrowed center of a ravine; here and there an aqueduct, a cabin, an abandoned mining claim, or a saw-mill, give variety to the ever changing landscape.

There will unfold new sights of natural grandeur to the admiration of the tourist winding his way through a series of beautiful forests, valleys, and glens, where on either side towering mountains solemnly look down upon the placid silver streams beneath. Sunshine alternates with shadow in the secluded recesses of a quiet mountain ravine, where clear crystal brooks run like silver

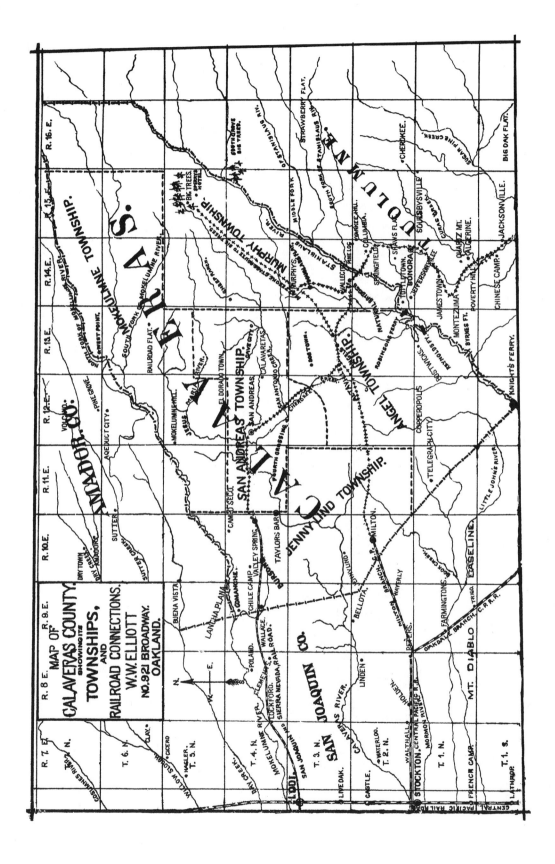

UPPER BRIDGE.

LOWER BRIDGE.

ELLIOTT. LITH, OAKLAND.

NATURAL BRIDGES OF CALAVERAS CO. CAL.
ON STAGE ROAD FROM BIG TREES TO YOSEMITE,
PROPERTY OF L.A. BARNES.

threads through the verdant landscape that they nourish. Admiration swells to enthusiasm before the sight of some rugged mountain standing like a sentinel at the summit of a narrow pass, that seems so high it might be presumed to reach the portals of the sky.

Over the wide and open valley game wing their flight, seeming to be poised still in the clear mountain air. It is the real play-ground for the sportsman. Through the thicket springs the light-footed deer, and the footprint of the bear is stamped on the ground. Foxes, silver-gray squirrels, rabbits, hare, mountain and valley quail, are in abundance here, and the clear brook streams contain the red-spotted trout, the mountain brook, and the salmon trout. When the sportsman wearies of the conquest with his gun, he can lay it aside for the rod and line, and, reclining in the shadow upon the brink of a bubbling brook, leisurely provide a finical feast of unexampled excellence.

In the agricultural view will be seen vast wheat fields; vineyards of the choicest grapes; the orange orchard; the largest fig-trees in the State. The valleys are rich with crops; there are cattle upon a thousand hills; the timber is of the finest kind, and the climate delightful. The visitor will acknowledge that Calaveras is by no means an unimportant county although not as well advertised as many others. Its agricultural products, its live stock, and its fruit trees make such a showing as prove it to be a great producer of the useful and valuable. Its undeveloped resources now being opened up by new railroad connection are almost inexhaustible.

RAILWAY PUSHING EASTWARD.

[From Lodi *Sentinel*.]

THE San Joaquin and Sierra Nevada Railroad is pushing its way eastward through Calaveras County, opening up at least 300,000 acres of United States Government lands subject, to-day, to entry, on which is found some of the best mineral lands in the States; besides, the foot-hills of Calaveras present the finest opening on the coast to men of small means, who desire to make homes for their families and engage in either fruit or wine culture. "Valley Springs," the present terminus, is at a distance of forty-one miles from Brack's Landing on the Mokelumne.

We understand that the company intends to push the road through to the Big Trees at the earliest practicable moment. It will connect the foot-hill and mountain homes with the valleys, and will infuse new life and energy into every branch of industry. New homes will spring up among them, new faces be seen and new associations will be formed. With these advantages, of course will come men with skill, with energy, with money; and we confidently predict that within ten years the foot-hills of Calaveras will be among the most populous and wealthy portion of our State.

A local paper says: "When the road is put in good order for travel and freight, the county will begin to brace up as the influence of the road in promoting our interests will become apparent. People will then begin to realize that Calaveras has some life still, when they actually feel the benefit and advantages to be derived by being brought in more direct communication with the outer world."

MAMMOTH GROVE HOTEL,

JAMES L. SPERRY, PROPRIETOR.

THE Grove Hotel having been enlarged can now accommodate one hundred guests. It has a laundry, hot and cold baths, a billiard table, bar, verandas, parlor, ball-room, the most pleasant sleeping apartments, and furnishes the best of fare at the table. It faces the grove, having the greater number of trees to the left, looking from the veranda, and the two "Sentinels" immediately in the front, about two hundred yards to the eastward. One of these is shown in our illustration of this delightful spot.

The valley in which this grove is situated

contains of the *Sequoia* trees, ninety-three, not including those of from one to ten years' growth. There are also hundreds of sugar and pitch pines of astonishing proportions, ranging to the height of 275 feet, and having not unfrequently a diameter of ten to eleven and a half feet. Anywhere else these pines would be regarded as vegetable monsters. Here, by the side of the *Sequoia*, they look like dwarfs.

There is good hunting ground in the vicinity mountain quail are abundant near by, and on the Stanislaus, three miles distant, grouse and deer abound. The San Antonio contains

THE SENTINELS.

trout of fine size. Delightful horseback or buggy rides conduct the visitor to many interesting points of scenery, or objects of curiosity, among which, besides the Falls of San Antonio, may be mentioned the Basaltic Cliffs on the North Fork of the Stanislaus River, and the Cave at Cave City, fifteen miles to the west, and the Natural Bridges near Vallecito.

During the summer and spring months this valley is exempt from the heat of the lower country and from the cold of the snow range. Vegetation blooms early in May, remaining fresh and green until the middle of October. The water is always pure and cold, and the hotel is furnished with ice all through the summer and autumn. Snow falls usually about the middle of December, and disappears from the grove entirely by the middle of April.

The Big Trees have been heard of wherever the photographic art is known, or the English language is spoken. This species of tree is known as the *Sequoia gigantea*, and was named in honor of Sequoia, a Cherokee Indian, who is supposed to have been born about 1770. The big tree is limited in its range, and is not so extensively found as the redwood. They are both a peculiarity of California, although a very few have been found across the border in Oregon. The big trees are found only in groves, while the redwoods cover extensive tracts.

Tourists, to visit these trees, leaving San Francisco, can take the Central Pacific Railroad to Stockton, and the Copperopolis Railroad to Milton, or the new narrow gauge railroad which connects with the Central at Lodi, thence to Valley Springs and San Andreas. Connection is made on either route with Matteson's daily line of stages, to the Big Trees. A daily coach leaves the Big Trees for Milton, connecting at Murphy's with a daily line to Yosemite Valley *via* Hutchings' new route, being the shortest and best.

THE CALAVERAS BIG TREES.

THE mammoth grove of big trees is situated in a small valley, near the headwaters of the San Antonio, one of the largest streams in central Calaveras, and five miles east of the falls of said stream, which are 150 feet in height, and surrounded by the grandest of scenery.

The grove is 4,585 feet above the level of the sea, and contains 10 trees, each one 30 feet in diameter, and over 70 of which

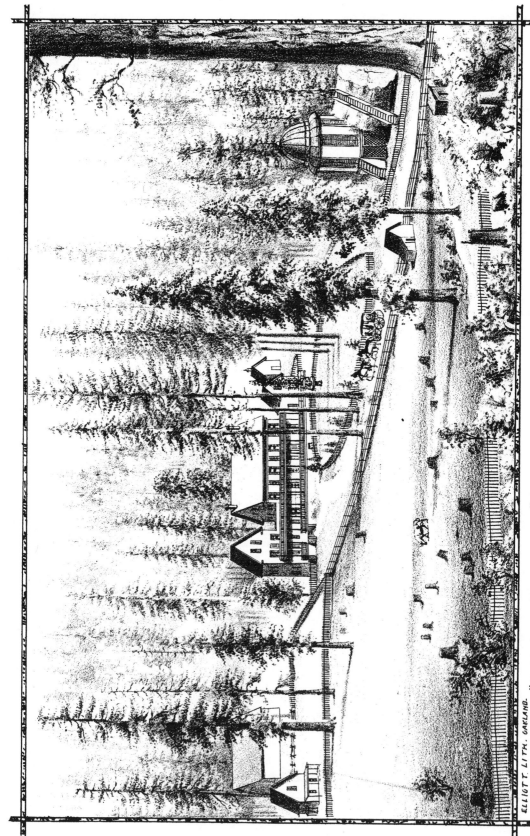

ELLIOTT. LITH. OAKLAND.

"MAMMOTH GROVE HOTEL", CALAVERAS BIG TREES, CALAVERAS CO. CAL.

PROPERTY OF JAMES L. SPERRY.

HOTEL OF F. MAYER.

WINE CELLAR.

VINEYARD, ORCHARD & RESIDENCE OF F. MAYER, MOKELUMNE HILL, CALIFORNIA.

are between 15 and 30 feet. Hittell, in his "Resources of California," says: "One of the trees which is down—'The Father of the Forest'— must have been 450 feet high, and 40 feet in diameter."

In 1853 one of the largest trees, 92 feet in circumference and over 300 feet high, was cut down. This tree employed five men for twenty-two days in felling it — not by chopping it down, but by *boring* it *off* with pump augers. After the stem was fairly severed from the stump, the upright ness of the tree, and the breadth of its base, sustained it in its position. To accomplish the feat of throwing it over, about two and a half days of the twenty-two were spent in inserting wedges, and driving them in with the butts of trees, until, at last, the noble monarch of the forest was forced to tremble, and then to fall, after braving " the battle and the breeze," for nearly three thousand years.

The stump of this tree has been smoothed off, and now easily accommodates thirty-two dancers. Theatrical performances have been held upon it, and in 1858 a newspaper, the *Big Tree Bulletin*, was printed there.

Near the stump lies a section of the trunk; this is 25 feet in diameter and 20 feet long; beyond lies the immense trunk as it fell, measuring 302 feet from the base of the stump to its extremity. Upon this was situated a bar-room and ten-pin alley, stretch- ing along its upper surface for a distance of 81 feet, affording ample space for two alley- beds, side by side.

About 80 feet from this stump stand the " Two Sentinels," each over 300 feet high, and the larger 23 feet in diameter. The carriage road approaching Sperry's Hotel passes directly between the "Two Sentinels," both very fine trees.

This " Big Tree Stump" not far from Sperry's Hotel is perfectly smooth, sound and level. Upon this stump, however incredible it may seem, on the 4th of July, thirty-two persons were engaged in dancing four sets of cotillions at one time, without suffering

any inconvenience whatever; and besides these, there were musicians and lookers-on. Across the solid wood of this stump, five and a-half feet from the ground (now the bark is removed, which was from fifteen to eighteen inches in thickness), it measures 25 feet, and with the bark, 28 feet. Think for a moment; the stump of a tree exceed- ing *nine yards* in diameter, and sound to the very center. There is a frame around the stump which forms the base of the house inclosing it. This is 93 feet and 7 inches in circumference at the ground. The spurs in some places project beyond the frame, while in others they are within it. This tree when standing was 302 feet high.

Another of these wonders, the largest tree now standing, which, from its immense size, two breast-like protuberances on one side, and the number of small trees of the same class adjacent, has been named the "Mother of the Forest." In the summer of 1854, the bark was stripped from this tree by Mr. George Gale, for purposes of exhibition in the East, to the height of 116 feet; and it now measures in circumference, without the bark, at the base, 84 feet; 20 feet from base, 69 feet; 70 feet from base, 43 feet 6 inches; 116 feet from base, and up to the bark, 39 feet 6 inches. The full circumference at the base, including bark, was 90 feet. Its height was 327 feet. The average thickness of bark was 11 inches, although in places it was about 2 feet. This tree is estimated to con- tain 537,000 feet of sound inch lumber. To the first branch it is 137 feet. The small black marks upon the tree indicate where auger holes were bored and rounds inserted by which to ascend the tree when removing the bark.

In the center of the grove is a tree 280 feet high, 17 feet in diameter, singularly hollowed out on one side by fire, and named "Pluto's Chimney." The "Chimney" made by the fire is on the north side, and extends from the ground 90 feet upward. One hun- dred feet north of the "Pioneer's Cabin," stand the " Quartette " cluster, the highest of which is 220 feet; and 50 yards east of this is a healthy young tree, 13 feet in diameter, and 250 feet high, and named in 1865 by a San Francisco lady, "America." It has been well-named.

A few steps further bring us to the "Fallen Monarch," the base section of a huge trunk, which has to all appearances been down for centuries. It is still 18 feet in diameter, although the bark and much of the wood have been wasted away by time. What is left is perfectly sound; but the upper half or two-thirds, which struck the earth with greatest force in its fall, has all disappeared, and trees nearly a century old are growing where it struck. This tree must have been over 300 feet high and 25 feet in diameter.

Further on standing near the uprooted base of the "Father of the Forest," the scene is grand and beautiful beyond description. The "Father" long since bowed his head in the dust, yet how stupendous even in his ruin! He measures 112 feet in circumference at the base, and can be traced 300 feet where the trunk was broken by falling against another tree; here it measures 16 feet in diameter, and according to the average taper of the other trees this venerable giant must have been 450 feet in height when standing. A hollow chamber or burnt cavity extends through the trunk 200 feet, large enough for a person to ride through. Near its base, a never-failing spring of water is found. Walking upon the trunk and looking from its uprooted base, the mind can scarce conceive its prodigious dimensions, while on the other hand tower his giant sons and daughters, forming the most impressive scene in the forest.

The burned-out tree in the grove called the "Pioneer's Cabin" has been cut through. The opening is now large enough to admit the passage of a loaded coach and horses. When it is taken into consideration that the tree is still alive and flourishing, it seems wonderful indeed.

SOUTH PARK GROVE OF BIG TREES.

ABOUT six miles from the Calaveras Grove just mentioned is the South Grove. This grove has over 1,300 *Sequoias* and is nearly two miles in extent. There is only a trail leading to this grove, and the route is through a very wild and romantic country. For a mile is traveled a beautifully wooded hill. Green dells, open to the sun-

HOLLOW IN BIG TREE.

shine, divided the grove of pines. The sky is pure and cloudless, clasping the landscape with a belt of peace and silence. Out of these woods after crossing the turnpike is reached the Divide and a beautiful view bursts upon our sight. The steep Sierra uplifts its craggy summits, white with drifts of snow (August 1st). In the distance rises a sublime chain of granite peaks, soaring far out of the region of trees and lifting its rocky summits into the sky. And far beyond, filling up the magnificent vista—filling up the lower steeps, crowned with pines—were the shining snows of the Dardanelle peaks,

RESIDENCE & HOTEL OF CAPT THOMAS B. MEADER, COPPEROPOLIS, CAL.

ELLIOTT LITH. OAKLAND. "MITCHLER'S HOTEL," MURPHYS, CAL. MRS. ELIZABETH MITCHLER & SONS, PROPR'S.

while long ranges of dark hills fade away behind each other with a perspective that hinted of the hidden peaks between. The path now leads through long, winding glens, overgrown with tall pines of two kinds, the yellow and the sugar pines. You catch but fleeting glimpses of the view through the trees and then, plunging into the forest, winding around the mountain side, suddenly exclaim: "There is a Big Tree!" There are so many wonderful ones that it is hard to describe them.

We would advise every lover of grand and beautiful scenes and sublime views to pay this grove a visit and judge for himself. It is well worth the trouble. One of the largest trees, called "New York," is over 400 feet high, 104 feet in circumference, and 34 feet in diameter. It surpasses all the standing trees in its size and its imposing grandeur.

"Smith's Cabin" is named after a hunter and guide, who lived in its burnt-out base for two years. The interior is 16 by 21½ feet. Its height is 340 feet. Here Smith weathered the terrible gale that was the downfall of "Old Goliah," his neighbor. During the progress of the hurricane he did not dare to venture out, as limbs and trees were constantly coming down. The fall of "Old Goliah" he compared to an earthquake. "Old Goliah" is the largest fallen tree in the grove; it measures, as it lies, 105 feet in circumference, and has a present length intact of 261 feet. A limb alone measures 12 feet in circumference. It required no stretch of the imagination to make it the deck of some long ship.

Sitting upon the upper part of the base of the tree we were 23 feet above ground. At 261 feet, where it is broken off, it measures 45 feet in circumference. It has also suffered from fire. Its base has been put to a highly practical use, being no less than a stable for horses. Scientific men of note pronounce the trees to be from two to four thousand years old, their age being judged by the number of circular woody rings they possess. That fire of one thousand years

ago raged among the *Sequoias* alone. Nor does this seem incredible, when vast sugar pines 27 and 30 feet in circumference and 250 feet high, now growing side by side with these trees, show no sign of fire, proving conclusively that they had no existence at that time. All the *Sequoias*, wherever found, show marks of fire. There are no exceptions among the old trees, as they and they alone had no existence then.

To get some comparative idea of the size of one of these largest fallen trees, let us suppose it laid in the street of some town. It would fill the street the length of four ordinary blocks of one hundred feet. At its base it would reach from sidewalk to sidewalk (forty feet). Those living in the third story of houses could not see over its trunk.

If these old giants could only answer two questions, How old are you? and, What were the conditions under which you grew? how much speculation, and how many theories would vanish into space. Probably at one time this was a dense forest of *Sequoias* and time alone has seen its fall and ruin, only these few giants remaining to tell the story.

FAMOUS MINING COUNTY.

CALAVERAS County is famous in the mining annals of the State. Abundant wealth, locked in the arms of the earth, has inspired long lines of men to explore its depths for the precious metals. The tunnels, drifts, and other devices for mining operations, to be seen in many places in the county, sufficiently indicate the struggle and mighty endeavor to bear away the gold from its natural home.

Gold was discovered before and in the days of 1849–50, and the yield of bullion has been large ever since. Quartz veins crop out of every hill, and nearly every town was started by the discovery of a mine. Among the windings of every creek and river bed may be found old Mexican arastras, many of them almost obliterated by time.

"In 1853," says J. M. Hutchins, " we saw

a large nugget of gold in shape like the kidney of an ox, that was dug out here, which weighed twenty-six pounds. It would have been ours but for the trifling circumstance,—didn't have the money to buy it!"

At another time one weighing twelve pounds was taken out, and was purchased by Morris Cohen, who is now a resident of San Francisco. And in 1858, there were several pieces taken out, of various sizes, weighing from one to five pounds.

SECTION OF THE MAMMOTH TREE.

It may be stated as an interesting fact that when Mr. Murphy, after whom the camp was named, left this camp to take up his residence at San Jose, California, he had as much gold as six mules could haul from the camp. In those early days, under extraordinary conditions, when provisions were scarce, coffee, tea, sugar, and tobacco were put in the scale with gold to balance, and sold pound for pound.

Carson Hill is celebrated for its unparalleled yield of the precious metals; and the history of gold mining does not afford like examples of the enormous production of ponderous masses of gold in a short time—$2,800,000 worth of gold was extracted in seven months, and from contiguous pits not 100 feet deep; $14,000 worth was taken out of a shaft in a day; and $20,000 worth out of another only 60 feet deep. The weight of the masses of gold was expressed in pounds, not in ounces; one mass of gold weighed 6½ pounds and another 7½ pounds.

But the most marvelous account of all is that of the blast in the Pacheco Shaft, which threw down a mass of rock so filled with gold that the masses held together when cracked by sledge hammers—one mass so broken out weighed 108 pounds and contained 104 pounds of gold. This is the largest mass of vein gold which has been found in the world, at least of which there is any record.

The mining resources of this section of country are too valuable to be ever neglected. Certainly they are too promising to be retarded because of lack of confidence in their outlook.

Hydraulic and channel mining meet with success if well managed. Marble, granite, limestone, iron, and coal have been discovered, and await capital and workmen for their development into new sources of prosperity.

LOCATION OF NUMEROUS TOWNS.

MILTON, in the southern part, is the terminus of the Stockton and Copperopolis Railroad. From the depot there provisions of all kinds are conveyed in large freight wagons to all parts, and this forms a profitable business to those engaged. From this point stage lines connect with all the principal towns and the counties

RESIDENCE OF JUDGE IRA. H. REED SAN ANDREAS. CAL.

ELLIOTT LITH. LITH. OAKLAND.

LIVERY & STAGE STABLE MURPHYS, CALAVERAS CO. CAL.

above. Hundreds of tourists pass through every year, making the stage companies rich and the livery business a profitable one. The pursuits of sheep-raising and farming are engaged in, to which the residents look for their chief support. Population, 120. It is 340 feet above sea level.

Sheep Ranch is the most modern town. It sprang up like a mushroom with the discovery of the American and Chavanne gold-quartz mines, and maintains its prosperity by their scientific development and permanent yield.

Carson Hill is upon the great leading quartz vein of the State of California, known generally as the Mother Vein, which is believed to extend from Mariposa to Grass Valley, a distance of over 100 miles. The vein varies from a few feet to 20 and 30 feet in thickness, and stands boldly out on the crest of the hill.

West Point is the extreme town on the northwest; Mokelumne Hill on the west center; Campo Seco, Comanche, Valley Springs, and Burson on the west; Jennie Lind and Milton on the southwest; Copperopolis and Telegraph City on the south; Altaville and Angel's Camp on the east center; Vallecito, Murphy's, and Sheep Ranch on the north-

east of the county, where all supplies for the central and eastern portions of the county are received and distributed; stage lines diverge to San Andreas, Sheep Ranch, Copperopolis, Angel's, Murphy's, the Big Tree groves, and Sonora.

PARADISE FOR THE HONEY BEE.

IN the spring the honey flora is of the greatest beauty and luxuriance. Here the apiarist and botanist might find delight in natural gardens of rainbow-tinted bloom, which are of almost endless variety. There are few apiaries in Calaveras County, though this is not the fault of its natural advantages, for although this superabundance of wild flora passes away by the middle of August, except along the creeks and moist places, where it flourishes until autumn, many shrubs and the rose-briers bloom until winter sets in. Those ranchers who have a few hives have an abundance of honey for their own use and have to devote but little attention to the bees. Such results should encourage this industry, especially since it can be carried on as an auxiliary to other business.

THE RETURNING CALAVERAS PROSPECTOR RELATES HIS EXPERIENCE.

FINE SUPPLY OF WATER.

THERE are three rivers in Calaveras, one from which the county takes its name, the Mokelumne and the Stanislaus, none of them very important, but all very useful.

The eastern border of the county is defined by the Stanislaus, while the Mokelumne River bounds the west, and the central portion is drained by the Calaveras River with its many tributaries. Water distributed by artificial means is used chiefly for mining

ASCENDING THE FALLEN MONARCH.

purposes, the agricultural interests at present requiring only small quantities.

The largest aqueduct constructed at present is the Mokelumne Hill and Seco Canal, which receives its water from the Mokelumne River. (See view of this canal.)

The Murphy Canal, or Union Ditch, receiving its water supply from the Stanislaus River, is nearly as important. Its waters are extremely fresh and pure, formed as they are from the melting snows of the mountains above drained by the Stanislaus; and its banks nearly the whole distance are embowered by alders, poplars, and vines, making the roadway between Murphy's and Big Trees, which is built upon its banks and

between giant-wooded hills, one of the most picturesque and beautiful in the State.

There are several smaller canals receiving water from the Calaveras River and its tributaries, and one of some importance is supplied from the Salt Spring Valley Reservoir, a beautiful sheet of water held in a natural depression of the valley by a strong earth dike extending several hundred feet. This vast water supply, if a reduction in its prices could be obtained, might be utilized by the horticulturist and manufacturer to such an extent as to become a source of immense wealth. Its fall, which is great from the east to the western border of the county, is utilized at present by some manufactories, but their operations are comparatively insignificant.

"SOCIETY UPON STANISLOW."

NO pre-historic remains have been reported as found within the present limits of the county, but stone mortars, pestles and arrow-heads have been found, according to reports, in Pliocean gravel, at Murphy's Camp Shaw's Flat, Columbia, Springfield, Tuolumne, Table Mountain, Sonora, and Knight's Landing. The fossil bones found are not numerous; and no large and valuable skeletons have been brought to light, but many fragments. None of the large saurians—those wonderful lizards, as large as whales of an early geological era—have yet been found here; but hills and mountains contain the bones of the mastodon, elephant, rhinoceros, hippopotamus, horse, camel, whale, and a quadruped resembling a tapir. Part of the skull of a man was found at the depth of 131 feet in

OFFICE & RES. OF M.K. REID, ED. of "MOUNTAIN ECHO" ANGELS CAL.

NORTH BRANCH STORE & P.O. OF W.R.TERRY. CAL.CO.

RUFE AND KEILBAR, MARKET. MURPHYS. CAL.

PUBLIC SCHOOL. ANGELS.CAL.

SCHOOL HOUSE, MURPHYS, CAL.

MOKELUMNE HILL SCHOOL HOUSE. CALAVERAS CO.CAL.

F. W. PEEK'S VARIETY STORE, MOKELUMNE HILL CAL.

RES. OF JAMES CREIGHTON, CAMPO SECO. CAL.

RES. & ORANGE GROVE OF GEO. W. CUTTER CAMPO SECO.

RES. OF F. H. DAY. MOKELUMNE HILL, CAL.

RES. OF E. E. BURCE. MOKELUMNE HILL, CAL.

sinking a shaft in the mines, under four successive strata of lava, which upsets the theory of geologists, that man did not exist at that age of the world.

But as an illustration of the uncertainty attending the identity of fossil remains reported to be discovered, we give the following lines from Brete Harte:—

"SOCIETY UPON THE STANISLOW."

I reside at Table Mountain, and my name is Truthful James;
I am not up to small deceit, or any sinful games;
And I'll tell in simple language what I know about the row
That broke up our society upon the Stanislow.

But first I would remark, that it is not a proper plan
For any scientific gent to whale his fellow-man,
And, if a member don't agree with his peculiar whim,
To lay for that same member for to "put a head" on him.

Now nothing could be finer or more beautiful to see,
Than the first six months' proceedings of that same society.
Till Brown of Calaveras brought a lot of fossil bones
That he found within a tunnel near the tenement of Jones.

Then Brown he read a paper, and he reconstructed there,
From those same bones, an animal that was extremely rare,
And Jones then ask'd the Chair for a suspension of the rules
Till he could prove that those same bones were one of his lost mules.

Then Brown he smiled a bitter smile, and said he was at fault,
It seemed he had been trespassing on Jones' family vault.
He was a most sarcastic man, this quiet Mr. Brown,
And on several occasions he had clean'd out the town.

Now I hold it is not decent for a scientific gent
To say another is an ass—at least, to all intent;
Nor should the individual who happens to be meant
Reply by heaving rocks at him to any great extent.

Then Abner Dean of Angel's raised a point of order—when
A chunk of old red sandstone took him in the abdomen,
And he smiled a kind of sickly smile, and curl'd up on the floor;
And the subsequent proceedings interested him no more.

For, in less time than I write it, every member did engage
On a warfare with the remnants of a palaeozic age;
And the way they heaved those fossils in their anger was a sin
Till the skull of an old mammoth caved the head of Thompson in.

THE POPULAR BIG TREE ROUTE.

THE most important and popular stage line in Calaveras County is by Matteson's Calaveras Big Tree route. By this line the visitor to the Big Trees enjoys the most comfort and freedom of mind from fear of accident, no other lines to the Big Trees being entirely under the management of one owner.

To take this route, from San Francisco, the tourist should purchase his ticket for Milton *via* the Central Pacific Railroad. At Milton he connects immediately with Matteson's stage which conveys him directly to the Big Trees. Any one desirous of visiting the Yosemite as well as the trees, cannot do better than to go from the trees by the same route *via* Sonora, connecting with the line running to the valley at Chinese Camp.

The stock and stages used on this line are excellent. Four-horse teams are used on all stages, and good time and close connections are the rule. It would be impracticable to fully describe the scenery and places through which this line passes, but a limited description cannot but be interesting to all.

Milton, the terminus of the Copperopolis Railroad, is a little town situated nearly at the commencement of the Sierra foot-hills. From Milton to Altaville, the next place of importance, the road passes through rural scenery and over picturesque hills from the summits of which some fine views of the grand snow-clad Sierras are obtained, towards which the spirited team is smartly traveling. From Altaville to Angel's is only one mile. Here the tourist sees numerous quartz mills, which are industriously pounding and grinding the precious rock, which is found so abundantly in the vicinity. From Angel's the stage passes on to Murphy's, taking the toll road called the Grade, an excellent highway passing through a wooded cañon. Murphy's is another mining camp, charmingly located. The road now approaches the heavy timber, which is soon reached, growing nobler and more abundant as altitude increases. A journey through this timber is most enjoyable, the atmosphere growing rarer and cooler as the journey progresses, the scent of the pines and the sighing of the breeze through their lofty boughs, the pleasant little farms with bright green meadows, which are occasionally passed —all tend to refresh and invigorate.

Finally Sperry's Big Tree Hotel is reached. The noble *Sequoias* are visited, affording no end of wonder. speculation, and discussion. After a stay here for a few days, the tourists who include the Yosemite in the trip return by the same road to Murphy's, whence they journey to Sonora and thus on to the valley. About seven miles from Murphy's they pass by the Natural Bridge, described and illustrated in this work, which we should not fail to visit.

Mr. Matteson also owns a fine livery stable at Murphy's, the subject of a full page view in this work. At full livery outfit is kept, which affords ample opportunity for parties seeking pleasure in that section so abounding in interest.

For tickets and information, apply to Thomas T. Walton, ticket agent, Yosemite Valley, or of Joseph Knowlton, Jr., ticket agent, 613 Market Street, San Francisco.

undulating hills of this county, Why it is that people of leisure will idle away hours of a brief life in the midst of grim, smoky, dusty towns, on the streets, sidewalks, in crowded saloons, halls, or theaters, when such a lovely panorama of nature can be seen at so little cost and trouble, is a mystery beyond comprehension.

One hour at present spent in our foot-hill country, listening to singing larks, beholding the fancifully variegated colors of the beautifully gorgeous flowers and verdure that cover the rolling wave like mounds, inhaling the delicious odors of nature's garden, drinking in,

FELLING BIG TREE FOR CENTENNIAL EXHIBITION.

FOOT-HILLS OF CALAVERAS.

(From *Stanislaus News.*)

A DRIVE among the foot-hills of Calaveras would, at this season of the year, amply repay the lover of nature. The lower ranges of gentle, smooth, rolling, treeless hills are covered with a complete mass of green vegetation, intercepted throughout with borders and beds of the loveliest of wild flowers of every hue, color, and shade of the rainbow. At this season of the year nature essays to deck our land in her loveliest attire, and nowhere under the sun is this more manifest than along the

under the calm sky, the pure health-giving atmosphere, should give a greater sense of joy to the mind than months in the crowded towns. Yet men, and even gentle women, never seem to think of enjoying the great and beautiful spectacle presented by nature free of cost. The invalid finds in the pure mountain atmosphere the healing which medicine fails to give, and the tourist perfect delight in the magnificent scenery and luxurious accommodations.

To the discouraged, dyspeptic, indigo colored, thin lipped, liver discolored, constipated inhabitant of towns, we recommend a week among the foot-hills.

RESIDENCE & STORE OF E PARKS, TELEGRAPH CITY, CAL.

THIS PROPERTY FOR SALE.

ELLIOTT, OAKLAND, CAL.

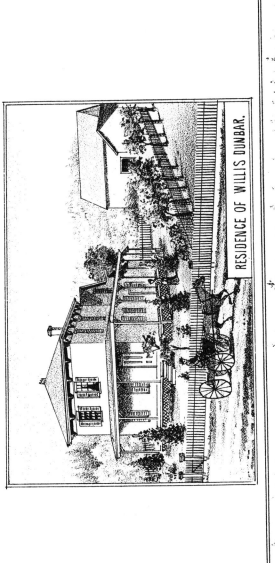

RESIDENCE OF WILLIS DUNBAR.

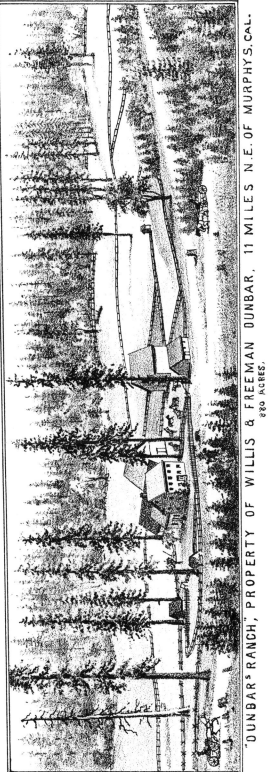

"DUNBAR'S RANCH," PROPERTY OF WILLIS & FREEMAN DUNBAR, 11 MILES N.E. OF MURPHYS, CAL.
880 ACRES.

THE RELIGIOUS INTERESTS OF CALAVERAS COUNTY.

BY REV. A. OSTROM.

IMMIGRANTS in selecting homes in a new country are anxious to know not only of its resources but of the social and religious institutions and influences that aid so largely in the discipline and culture of the family.

Calaveras County, because of its rugged and broken surface, will never be occupied by large land-holders and extensive farmers, or stock-raisers, but will furnish multitudinous homes for fruit-growers, vine-dressers, and small farmers, and the constantly increasing numbers of this class indicate and foreshadow the growing prosperity of the county.

Intending emigrants will attach a special importance to the religious institutions of the county because of their refining and enabling influence on their families and homes.

The religious interests of Calaveras County are in charge of three religious denominations.

1. The Roman Catholic Church has a priest stationed at San Andreas. Rev. A. Geyer is the present incumbent He conducts services at appointed times in the following places in the county, viz.: San Andreas, Mokelumne Hill, Sheep Ranch, Eldorado, Murphy's, Angel's, Camp Seco. and Comanche. A Sabbath-school is connected with each of these fields.

2. The Methodist Episcopal Church North is the denomination which formerly had charge of work in many of the principal places in the county. They now own a parsonage in Mokelumne Hill, and supply that place with occasional service through their minister stationed at Jackson, Amador County. West Point is also supplied with occasional service by a Methodist minister stationed in Amador County.

A minister of the Methodist Episcopal Church South, located in San Joaquin County, holds occasional service at Milton.

A community of Dunkards, located in the chaparral district in the western portion of the county, hold among themselves occasional Sabbath services.

3. The Congregational denomination has a missionary stationed at Murphy's. He holds regular service at Murphy's, Douglas Flat, Vallecito, Angel's, Altaville, Copperopolis, Camp Seco, Valley Springs, and San Andreas, and occasional service at Salt Spring Valley, Milton, Eldorado, Calvaritas, Sheep Ranch, and Mokelumne Hill.

In connection with this work there are organized churches at Murphy's, Douglas Flat, Copperopolis, San Andreas, and Sheep Ranch.

Good Sabbath-schools are connected with the organized churches and at most of the places where occasional service is held. Sabbath-schools are maintained during the larger part of the year. This work is at present in charge of Rev. A. Ostrom, a member of the General Association of California, and an agent of the American Home Missionary Society. He is stationed at Murphy's.

Rev. Thomas Kirkland, of San Francisco, has been appointed to co-operate with him in this field, and will probably be stationed at San Andreas.

MURPHY'S CAMP.

THIS was at one time one of the leading mining camps. It is situated at an elevation of 2,400 feet above the level of the sea and in a gold basin of extraordinary richness. It was named after Martin Murphy, its discoverer, who took out an immense amount of gold. The hills, gulches, gorges and small valleys in the vicinity of this camp have been tunneled, cut, scalped and literally torn to pieces by the energy of man seeking to wrestle from nature its coveted gold. The zeal of the miner appears to have been supported by the assurance that the metal was in the earth, and that only his want of energy kept him from its possession. "Terrific rich" is how the country folks express their idea of the district, and they have the obvious corroboration of their views upon all sides.

This part of the county, from Murphy's to San Andreas, a distance of about twenty-five miles, is well adapted to vine and fruit raising. The vine and fruit tree are in cultivation by a large number of the people, and the introduction of an abundant supply of water will give a marvelous impetus to this industry. There is plenty of room for active and honest workers here, and the future promise of this section of country from the fruit and vine growth cannot be overestimated. In fact there can be no exaggeration of the value of the vine and fruit interests.

The town is built in a forest of pine, and along the streets are planted ornamental trees. In Murphy's there are many magnificent orchards and vineyards; the fruit has a fine flavor and is of extraordinary size. Fruit trees are very thrifty, even young trees flourishing to a goodly degree the first year; apples, pears, quinces, figs, pomegranates, peaches, apricots, and other kinds of fruit do well. This section of the foot-hills might become the vast orchard of the State on account of the abundance of pure water and mountain climate. Also around this portion of the State in the vicinities of Copperopolis, Angel's, San Andreas, Murphy's, and, in fact, in almost every part of this county, there are good tracts of land to be pre-empted, and fit for raising hay, grain, vegetables and fruits, besides serving for pasture lands when uncultivated. Murphy's is one of the most lovely towns in the county. It is situated at

such an altitude that the air is very pure, clear and invigorating, and it makes even distant objects appear near.

CAMP LIFE IN CALAVERAS.

CALAVERAS is a great resort for campers who leave the dry, hot valleys with their families and live in the fragrance and grandeur of the pines and big trees. They seek to find rest and recreation away from the constant toil and pressure of business.

RIDING THROUGH THE FALLEN KING.

California offers special advantages for camp life. The rains will have generally ceased about the 1st of May, and for the six months thereafter everything has become so dry that no danger need ensue from sleeping out in the open air. Besides one has a variety of climates to choose from. Those who like a temperature rugged and bracing will find it along the coast. By going a distance in the interior, the ocean winds are shorn of their moisture, the middle of the day being very warm, but the mornings and evenings are truly delightful. But it is higher up in the Sierra Mountains that we find the

SCHOOL HOUSE.

STORE & RESIDENCE of S. A. PERRY & SONS, DOUGLAS FLAT, CAL.

ELLIOTT LITH. OAKLAND CAL.

OFFICE OF CALAVERAS CITIZEN, SAN ANDREAS, CAL.
C. R. BEAL, ED. & PROP'R.

UNION LIVERY STABLE J.F. WASHBURN, PROPR. SAN ANDREAS.

RES. OF GEO. KELTON, BIG BAR, ON MOKELUMNE RIVER, CAL.

OFFICE OF THE CALAVERAS PROSPECT. GETCHELL & SALCIDO PROPS. SAN ANDREAS. CAL.

best climate. Here the atmosphere is pure and just suited to please the strong and bring comfort to invalids.

To one who has traveled over this State and noted the topography of the country, it is evident that California is truly a camper's paradise. The roads are generally well graded and easy of access. We will take first as an illustration the two largest valleys of the State, the Sacramento and San Joaquin. They are so easy in grade that one can travel 500 or 600 miles in one direction over roads as level as the floor. Contiguous to them are a number of smaller valleys that afford many a delightful spot to pitch a camper's tent. The soil is dotted with great park-like groves of live and white oaks and sycamores, with beautiful wild flowers growing profusely upon hillside and plain. Striking some of these valleys at their mouth, and ascending to their sources in the mountains, we come to rippling streams of water, shown in the engraving, flowing through tangled masses of trees and shrubs. They afford a good retreat to those who seek to place as good a distance as possible between them and the outside world; and when they return again to mingle with the people it will be with quickened blood and vigorous impulse.

Those who delight to pass their time with rod and gun will find that camp life will afford them the full measure of their wants in this respect. The mountain streams are alive with the speckled beauties that nip so charmingly at the treacherous bait. Hares of wonderful swiftness of foot and delicious eating abound on every side. Then the gentle dove furnishes a dish fit for a king. If you wish to try your gun on larger game, the coyote, beaver, wild cat, lynx, California lion and silver-gray fox will test the shooting abilities to the utmost. But it is the quail and deer that whet the appetite of the camper. He would consider his expedition barren in its results if he did not add these trophies of the chase to the walls of his tent. If he should desire to have a bear skin, let him ascend higher up in the mountains, and bruin will give him a tussle.

Let one of the company be selected as a leader, and his orders should be obeyed implicitly. Take nothing with you but what is absolutely necessary. You are going away for rest and pleasure, and the movements should be as free as possible. A person need have little fear of reptiles, as they are found only in the roughest spots, and are rarely dangerous if let alone. Do not let the restrictions of fashion hinder your seeking enjoyment, but do anything rational according to your own judgment. By entering into the spirit of the occasion, you will come back a new person, both in body and mind.

CATTLE RAISING IN CALAVERAS.

(By M. B. D., in S. F. *Chronicle*.)

THERE are few, if any, thoroughbred cattle raised, but among the large herds there are many good milk cows selling at average prices from $30.00 to $50.00, and sometimes as high as $75.00 or $90.00 a head. There are a number of dairymen making quiet little fortunes from the butter produce of their cattle, driving them to Alpine County in the dry season, and in this way pasturing them two-thirds of the year upon green feed, which gives to the butter a beautiful golden color and a sweetness highly prized. Large numbers are sold as beef cattle, at present bringing 10 or 12 cents per pound.

Cattle raising is one of the oldest industries. More than thirty years ago those hills were ranged by the bold Spanish and Mexican riders, mounted upon fierce little mustangs, in pursuit of their wild long-horned charges, and to-day in the more unsettled portions, especially in the South and West, there still remain vaqueros as intrepid and bold as the notorious Texas cowboys.

At present sheep have taken the place of cattle raising to a great extent and they do well, their wool and mutton bringing prices as high as those of any other section. Wild animals, a small gray wolf, catamounts and coyotes, long have proved a source of loss, but shepherds have greatly reduced this evil.

Swine raising is rather an industry of the past than of the present. Ten years ago the hills were covered with good specimens of this animal and they found an abundance of food in the wild acorn crops and in the many varieties of bulbous roots. Pork raised here was famous for the delicacy of its flavor, and it has not deteriorated in this respect, for some of the higher and unfrequented hills are still inhabited by what are called wild hogs, and their flesh is preferred to fat venison by

COURT HOUSE SAN ANDREAS.

many. Poultry, when well cared for, does remarkably well, and every ranch has its poultry yard, producing first-class fowls, turkeys and eggs, which always find a ready market in Stockton or San Francisco, where they are usually shipped for sale.

One of the principal interests of Calaveras County is grazing. The land is covered with a wild vegetation of many varieties, growing in abundance and of nutritious quality. It sprouts with the early autumn rains and by December is fit for grazing purposes. The herds find generally sufficient support without being fed hay or grain at any season, unless in unusually stormy winters. The wild oat

grows so luxuriantly in some small alluvial spots that it is cut for hay. Between the rocky masses that frown upon the hills these wild oats form beautiful turfs and fringes, tempting cattle to climb to the very summits for it, and it lasts the whole year, drying to a pale yellow with the drought of summer and being pushed aside by the tender shoots of the next spring. Much of the land is valuable chiefly for grazing purposes, and supports thousands of sheep and cattle most of the year.

Herds from the San Joaquin Valley are pastured here for a season. The unoccupied land also is used for pastoral purposes, there being a sort of common agreement that each shall respect the rights of his neighbor, and trespasses seldom occur. During the summer drought bands of sheep and cattle are driven from here to the green pastures of Alpine County above, and return before the winter sets in. The roads are made deep with dust by their numberless feet, and many times during the summer days the lowing of cattle or bleating of sheep, with the sound of their tinkling bells and the shouts of the herders, break upon the ear and form a picturesque scene.

FINELY LOCATED RANCH.

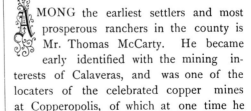MONG the earliest settlers and most prosperous ranchers in the county is Mr. Thomas McCarty. He became early identified with the mining interests of Calaveras, and was one of the locaters of the celebrated copper mines at Copperopolis, of which at one time he was the principal owner. The depression

C. R. LLOYD'S GENERAL MERCHANDISE STORE, SAN ANDREAS CAL.

METROPOLITAN HOTEL. SAN ANDREAS CAL. B.F. HAWES. PROPR.

PHOENIX LIVERY STABLE, P. MASTERSON PROPR. SAN ANDREAS, CAL.

SCRIBNER'S STORE. ANGELS, CAL.

RESIDENCE OF J. C. SCRIBNER, ANGELS. CAL.

of the market for copper and the consequent stoppage of the reduction works, brought financial distress upon many, among which Mr. McCarty suffered severely. With characteristic energy he turned his attention to farming, and has now one of the finest located foot-hill ranches in the county. It is situated in what is known as Salt Spring Valley, about four miles from Copperopolis.

Mr. McCarty is well versed in mining matters, and has a fund of information on all subjects relating to the interests of the county. He has large flocks of sheep and deals in other stock quite extensively. A view of this place appears on another page, giving only a partial idea of this beautiful place, but shows the timber and foot-hills of the background. The farm is well watered by a stream of water and several springs. There is an abundance of timber. The owner is one of the pioneer settlers, having arrived in California at an early day and settling in Calaveras County, with which he has been prominently identified.

CLIMATIC ADVANTAGES OF CALAVERAS COUNTY.

A SALUBRIOUS and pleasant climate prevails in Calaveras for at least ten months of the year. The altitude is from 1,200 to 1,800 feet above the sea level, and during the summer months the thermometer registers from seventy-five to one hundred degrees, and from February to March from thirty to seventy-five degrees above zero.

The purity and dryness of the air counteract the force of the heat and give a mildness to the climate, where a moist atmosphere would simply intensify the warmth. The nights have a refreshing coolness, and are usually without wind or fog. People afflicted with throat or lung diseases will find this section of country a desirable abode for pleasure or work. Untold numbers of pine and cedar trees raise themselves from the thick undergrowth upon the foot-hills. The air is balmy with the odor of these woods, and it is indeed delightful as well as healthful to spend the summer months in the mountains of Calaveras among its numerous unrivaled natural scenery.

The summers may be warm, and the mercury in the thermometer may linger lovingly around the 100 degree mark, but the farmer may hoe his corn, and the merchant may proceed about his business without danger of sun-stroke; and when the night comes it brings with it cooling breezes which make slumber refreshing.

MOUNTAIN HOMES.

THEY are to be found in all the old mining towns, sparkling gems, glistening upon the western slope of her eternal Sierra. The cozy, modest cottages, painted white, with old-fashioned green blinds; five, ten, twenty, forty, or eighty-acre tracts, surrounded by picket fences white as snow; flower gardens, such as can be seen nowhere else; trees with propped-up branches loaded down with fruit; beds of strawberries and blackberries, with gooseberry, currant and raspberry bushes clinging inside the fence in every direction; the magnificent patch of glorious California vegetables,—all are adjuncts of many a Calaveras home.

Some fifteen years since there was a man at Mokelumne Hill who went down the river to a point near Lancha Plana, and having selected a piece of land then covered with chaparral, commenced to grub and clear it off. He was absolutely the laughing-stock of the community. He kept on, however, and, having fenced his land, planted vines and trees, and for many years has had a most beautiful place, his fruit being of the very best quality, all of it finding a ready sale.

The foot-hills of California constitute the very best fruit and vineyard land in the State, and can be purchased at present at from about two and one-half to five dollars per acre, and, in many cases, be pre-empted.

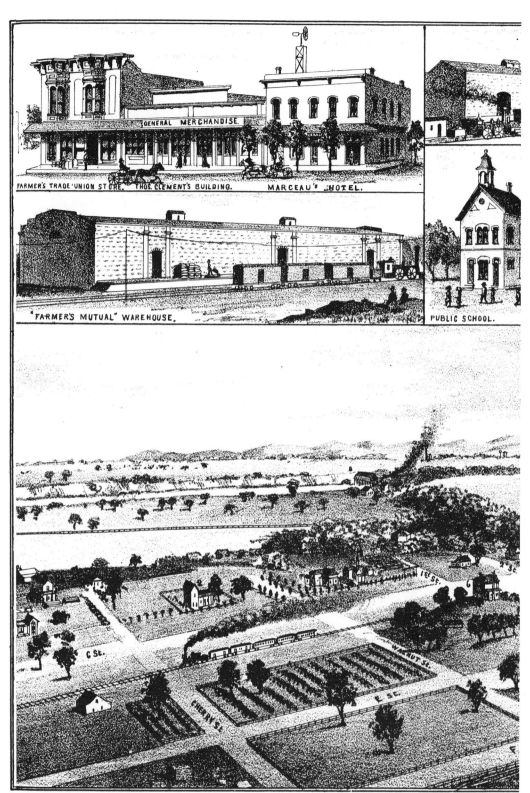

FARMER'S TRADE UNION STORE. THOS. CLEMENT'S BUILDING. MARCEAU'S HOTEL.

GENERAL MERCHANDISE.

PUBLIC SCHOOL.

"FARMER'S MUTUAL" WAREHOUSE.

C St.

1 RES. MRS. TICE & MISS CLEMENTS.	5 S. L. MAGEE.	9 CLEMENTS' PAVILION.
2 N. TOWNSEND.	6 J. A. ANDERSON.	10 J. W. BAKERS BLACKSMITH SHOP
3 J. W. BAKER.	7 CHAS. POPPE.	AND J. F. JENKINS' WAGON SHOP.
4 CHAS. SIEGEL.	8 MOKELUMNE RIVER BRIDGE.	11 FARMERS TRADE UNION.

CLEMENTS,
CAL

CLEMENTS WAREHOUSE.

LIVERY STABLE

RES. OF MRS. A.C.TICE & MISS M. CLEMENTS.

RESIDENCE OF J.A. ANDERSON.

CHAS. POPPE'S LIVERY STABLE.

LONE STAR MILL.

SAN JOAQUIN CO.
IFORNIA.

12 THOS. CLEMENTS STORE.   16 FARMERS MUTUAL WAREHOUSE.   20 CLEMENTS HOP HOUSE.
13 MARCEAUS' HOTEL.   17 ATHEARN SCHOOL HOUSE.   21 LONE STAR MILL.
14 CLEMENTS WAREHOUSE.   18 CLEMENTS RESERVOIR.
15 S.J. & S.N.R.R. DEPOT.   19 BRICK YARD.

ELLIOTT. LITH. OAKLAND.

WHAT CALAVERAS PRODUCES.

WHEAT, corn, oats and barley yield profitable crops, and there are vast quantities of hay raised. Thousands of tons are sold every season from one valley. Some of the finest ranches in the county raise hay in large quantities, as well as affording pasture for sheep and cattle.

STARTED FOR THE CALAVERAS DIGGINGS.

The fruit interest is undeveloped as yet, although there is promise of success in the future. Statistics show that the county contains less than 500 acres of vineyard altogether. The grapes raised here are of fine size and flavor, do not require more attention than grapes elsewhere, and make exceptionally fine raisins and wine. The wine especially is delicious in flavor, lacking the heavy and earthy taste sometimes complained of in the valleys. Because of the superior qualities of the grapes, viticulture should be greatly encouraged.

Apples, peaches, figs, pears, and plums, as well as all varieties of common vegetables, are successfully cultivated, though as yet in comparatively small orchards and gardens. The fruit is remarkable for its choice flavor, and the crop is seldom, if ever, blighted. Pomegranates, almonds, and all varieties of berries, bear well and seldom fail.

From the return of cereal crops of California for 1884, published in the Sacramento *Bee*, we learn that Calaveras County produced as follows:—

Cereals.	Acreage.	Yield.	Average.
Corn........	2,100	54,600	26
Wheat	27,000	324,000	12
Barley	11,000	198,000	18
Oats........	800	16,000	20
Total acreage.	40,900		

The above figures for yield are in bushels, and may be reduced to centals. Wheat, 60 pounds; barley, 47; oats, 32.

NATURAL BRIDGES OF CALAVERAS.

THE Upper Natural Bridge of Calaveras County is located 3 miles from Vallecito, and 500 yards from stage road leading from Calaveras Big Trees to Yosemite. Unlike all the other natural bridges known in the world, the two of Calaveras County, California, are a gradual formation from crystal spring water, requiring countless ages to attain their present magnitude and grandeur, one writer estimating it 42,000,000 of years. This, however, is but conjecture; it is evident that the spring was flowing down and parallel with the creek on the east side for many centuries before the bridge commenced forming. It is also evident that the bridge commenced forming at the upper or north end, forming across then down the stream. The spring water forms a coating on everything with which it comes in contact, heavy and hard as marble, but void of grit or ice until it reaches the level of the waters of the creek where it ceases to leave any trace. Positive measurement of 20 years' increase shows a trifle less than ⅛ of an inch. There is great reason to believe the mountain to the east is one great cavern containing a large subterranean lake which the proprietor hopes soon to open and explore.

This bridge varies from 12 to 76 feet breadth of span, from 8 to 40 feet high, and 240 feet through underneath the arch. To see its beauty and magnificence, visitors must pass through underneath. It has no equal in the world. Underneath the bridge, worn in the solid marble, are seven basins, or tanks, round, smooth, and true, as if measured with square and compass, and turned by rule. The two smaller ones, always in view, side by side, named the "Old Bach's and Old Maid's Wash Bowls," are one foot in diameter and one foot in depth; the others, in the center of the stream, are filled with water, rocks, and sand, varying from 4 feet diameter and 5 feet in depth to 23 feet diameter and 27 feet depth. Here is a study for scientific men. It is positive that the basins were worn before the flow of gold began.

As you go under this bridge, you first enter a large circular space 76 feet in diameter and from 8 to 16 feet high. In one corner, as it were, hangs what has been named the "Rock of Horeb," from which flows a living stream to refresh the thirsty visitor. Here the eye can feast for hours upon the over-hanging wonders, never tiring. Passing the partition, which is 6 feet high, the span becomes narrower, the arch rising to a height of 40 feet, and hung in rich sparkling festoons, charms the vision of the beholder. Directly overhead is called the pulpit, where eight persons have sat at a time, singing for hours, listening to the echo of the voices resounding from wall to wall, charming the ear.

Passing on to the right is "Lover's Retreat," where many a tender pair have uttered tender words but could not be seen to blush. We next enter the Gothic dining room. In this

chamber, upon entering it, the Right Rev. Father Leclera exclaimed, " I have visited everything great and wonderful in the whole *world* that I have ever heard or read of except Calaveras Big Trees, and am on my way to them, but [clasping hands and, with a reverential smile, looking to the ceiling above] this is the masterpiece of Nature."

A little further, and to the right hand, is the "Infant's Bath Tub," standing full of holy water, in which the Old Bach intends to immerse his first born. Still further on, also to the right, is the "Old Bachelor's Trap," where many a girl has paid toll for crawling through it.

Nearly opposite, and thirty feet high, is the "Bridal Chamber," which the Old Bach once entered alone; he remained but a short time, being so lonely; he descended and removed the ladder, resolving never to enter again until he was old enough to build a golden ladder, and enter in with his bride, pulling the ladder up after them. No pen can describe this vast arch so that one can realize it. No artist's pencil can portray its real beauty; it must be seen to be appreciated. Although but little known heretofore, it stands, nevertheless, without a rival in the world, the great masterpiece of Nature's handiwork. Our artists have given some sketches of the bridge, but its beauties can never be sketched.

Leaving the upper bridge we travel down the stream 540 yards, then enter the lower bridge. The first point noted on the left is the "Bridal Chamber," where it is supposed Adam and Eve spent their honey moon. It now appears cold and deserted although in close proximity to, and directly facing the "Devil's Oven," in which things are generally supposed to be kept warm. This name was given the place by the first party of miners who ever visited the bridge. A vast dome on the right resembles a huge baker's oven, hence the name. Passing down and to the left, is the "Baptismal Fount," being a level surfaced tank entirely of the same formation as the bridge, 6 feet long, 3 to 5 feet wide, and 18 inches deep, always full of crystal

RESIDENCE OF W. O. CUTLE

, JENNY LIND, CALIFORNIA.

ELLIOTT. LITH. OAKLAND.

water. Passing on and to the left is a large cove called the " Miner's Cabin," in which lived for nine summers a company of miners while working in the creek. Passing out from under the bridge, and turning around, the eye meets a view that baffles all description. Unlike the upper bridge, this one in its formation rises and projects outward, overhanging the stream, having many small open-

" PLENTY OF GOLD HERE, BOYS!"

ings or caverns, some of which have been entered a distance of 30 feet. From this point can be taken one of the finest stereoscopic views in the world. This bridge is 180 feet through underneath the arch, from 12 to 45 feet breadth of span, and from 6 to 15 feet high. This bridge is positively known to have formed from the water flowing from the mouth of an enormous cave, the entrance of which was over 150 feet high, and the width supposed to be from 60 to 80 feet; the water,

when coming to the light and heat, evaporating, forms a crust, sloping back with the surface of the mountain. This crust is, apparently, from 6 to 10 feet thick. The proprietor intends blasting away this crust formation, opening the cave for the travel of 1886.

The mountain to the east and southeast, ¾ of a mile distant, is known to have 10 or 15 caves on the summit, all being connected and having but this one outlet. Two of these caves have been partially explored by means of a rope, going down 300 feet. To this depth were chambers on either side, the extent of which is unknown. At this point lights were lowered with twine, but no bottom or limit on either side could be found, showing the chamber or cavern to be immense. One of the caves can be entered to a depth of 150 feet, being on an incline of 45 degrees; here were 3 small but beautiful chambers in which lived a man for 6 weeks, escaping the sheriff's search in 1859. From this point, descending 300 feet with rope, the whole mountain appears honeycombed with innumerable chambers which were not explored, from this point, and in the other caves no bottom could be found This adventure, however, came near proving fatal to one of the party. While one remained below to steady the rope from swinging, it was not difficult for the others to climb out, but when the last man attempted to climb, the rope began swaying from side to side and he slid back many times. The blood of the whole party curdled at the thought of his situation. We tried pulling the rope; it would not move over the jagged edge of the rock on which it hung; the fear also of cutting the rope, as it made so many vibrations as he attempted to climb, filled every breast with horror. After two hours' rest, which seemed to us as many days, he at last succeeded in reaching the top, where two strong men with superhuman strength each grasped an arm, and landed him, apparently lifeless from exhaustion. Not one of that party will ever be induced to repeat that trial of exploration.

When this cave was first discovered, no musical hall could excel it in melody. Having entered it to the 150 level with musicians, who in a few minutes with only a pocket knife played as sweet music as ever came from a piano upon the stalactites hanging from the ceiling. These have since been broken off by vandal hands, giving one that has seen it in its native beauty a feeling of solemnity on entering the place as it now appears. When the proprietor succeeds in opening these caves, not one human being will ever be allowed to enter the place until he has first recorded his name to an obligation not to scratch, write, or in any way disfigure them.

It has often been said by tourists that California contains more great natural wonders than any section of the world. It can also be said with equal truth that Calaveras County contains more than any county in the State.

FRUIT AND GRAPES.

[From Calaveras *Prospect.*]

IT is well known that the soil of the Calaveras foot-hills is unquestionably adapted for the cultivation of the grape, and fruit trees. We are earnestly of the opinion that when the S. J. and S. N. R. R. shall have crossed the county and tapped the timber belt, all that section for miles in the vicinity of Altaville, Angels, Vallecito, Douglas and Murphy's, through which a system of irrigation can be easily carried, will be transformed, as if by magic, into magnificent and luxuriant vineyards and orchards. While the mineral resources will be undergonig additional development the agricultural interests will not lie dormant; but the miner and the farmer will toil almost side by side. Each will profit by the labor of the other, and the prosperity of the county will be enhanced by the combined labors of both. Under its weekly leader, entitled the "Condition of the State," the *Bee* makes the following observation:—

The season of 1885–86 will probably show a much greater acreage planted in vines and fruit trees than any other season in the history of the State up to the present period. The advantages of fruit-culture, in comparison with the production of cereals, never before received such attention from the press. A great number of farmers, hitherto engaged exclusively in the production of grain, have become greatly dissatisfied with the meager returns from cereals, and have turned their attention to fruit. The expected reduction of overland freights has given a great impetus to the business of fruit-growing. While prices may be expected to decline to a considerable extent in the next few years, there need be no fear of overproduction, if good judgment be exercised in planting orchards and vineyards. Those who grow for the Eastern market, selecting such fruits as thrive better in California than anywhere else in the United States, can scarcely fail of a rich reward.

Large profits have been realized upon lands that were considered only just two years ago as practically valueless, and had no established practical value in our cities; while to-day, thanks to the wise and energetic course of the *Bee* and several other of the valley and bay papers, capitalists are offering to effect loans, when needed, of from $8.00 to $10.00 per acre upon good lands.

Tens of thousands of acres in our foot-hills of equally and desirable land are awaiting the active and enterprising settlers who have sufficient pluck to undertake its clearing and planting.

RESIDENCE OF ANSIL DAVIS,

DOUGLAS FLAT, CAL.

ELLIOTT, LITH. OAKLAND CAL.

THE TIMBER BELT.

ABOUT seven miles above Murphy's, the heavy timber belt commences, and spreads its flourishing growth widely and thickly, until the whole of this section is as dense as a tropical forest, with the sugar pine, the yellow pine, the spruce, fir, and cedar. The day is close at hand when this lumber region will be sought after and profitably utilized, and its valuable

WORKING THEIR CLAIM.

woods enjoy large sales in the valleys below and at Sacramento, Stockton, and San Francisco. Their market value need not be dwelt on here. They can always have a ready sale at good figures. Thus it will be seen at a glance that this county affords an additional source of business activity in its luxuriant growth of pine, spruce, fir, and cedar.

The timbered belt for grandeur, extent, diversity, and magnificent proportions, has no parallel in the entire timber belt of the western slope of the Sierras. Such is the opinion of all who have visited and traveled through this wonderfully profuse bounty of nature. This entire belt, during the summer and early fall months, is occupied by the pastoral population.

The San Joaquin and Sierra Nevada Railroad, now being rapidly constructed, has for one of its objects the reaching of this timber.

The hill slopes and plateaus are covered with forests of oak and pine and shrub growth. White oak prevails among this species and grows to a good size. It is cut in large quantities for four-foot wood and is of considerable value to land owners. In places, portions of land which are valuable chiefly for this wood, are robbed of their wealth by some squatter, who takes up a homestead or pre-emption claim for this purpose, and then leaves it valueless to those who might have improved it properly. The blue or nut pine prevails in the southern and western parts of the country, but is not a valuable timber.

The shrub growth is composed of chaparral, manzanita, poison oak, buckeye, and other varieties. They form a protection for stock in the winter storms and summer heats, and are used largely for fencing purposes by the ranchers. Some of the ridges are covered with a dense growth of chemissal (*Adenosloma*), a dark evergreen shrub which is of little value but of very beautiful appearance, especially when viewed from a distance. Then its shaded folds and sunlit loops seem like a rich silken plush.

That immense timber belt extending along nearly the whole distance of the Sierra Nevada Mountains, on the western slope, here culminates (in the higher foot-hills) with that gigantic grove, the Big Trees of Calaveras, so famous for the wonderful size of its trees.

This sylvan vegetation is composed of pine, the yellow or pitch pine taking the place of the blue of lower altitudes, with fir, cedar, and other trees adaptable to lumbering purposes, besides the species known to science as *Sequoia gigantea*, which forms the mammoth tree grove. The lumber interest is improved to some extent, though not as much as it might be. Along the perpetual water-courses grow alders, poplars, and black oaks, their giant branches festooned by wild grapevines and honeysuckles, while at their roots cluster clumps of wild blackberries and gooseberries, which bear fruit of good size and flavor.

CALAVERAS COUNTY.

[By Miss M. B. Davis, in S. F. *Chronicle.*]

ON the western slope of the Sierra Nevada Mountains, among the foot-hills, is Calaveras County. Its situation is one of the most advantageous in the State; it is central, easy of access, and possesses an admirable climate. In area it comprises about 1,000 square miles, and has a population, according to the last census, of over 9,000. Its surface is formed of long hill slopes and alluvial valleys, several small plateaus, and a ridge of sharp, rocky peaks in the eastern portion, reaching an altitude of 2,000 feet; and it is drained by a perfect network of rivers and creeks.

Its soil generally is composed of a light, reddish loam, and is deep only in places, the bed-rock appearing upon every hill-top and principally forming the higher peaks. The bed-rock is a coarse, grayish stone, interspersed with strata of more valuable rock, such as limestones, slate, and veins of different ores. The higher foot-hills are often capped with large deposits of lava and other volcanic materials.

Among these hills interesting fossils have been found—the bones of the mastodon, elephant, and other gigantic animals, with those of lesser mammals and land and fresh-water shells. One of these hills, Table Mount-ain, rising in steep precipitous walls above the Stanislaus River, is one of the great natural curiosities in the State. It is divided by the river, one part being in Tuolumne County. It extends a length of 30 miles, and its perfectly flat top is nearly 2,000 feet in width.

The climate of the county is one of the most healthful and delightful in the world, owing to the rare purity of the atmosphere. Although the thermometer reaches as high as 112 degrees Fahrenheit in midsummer, the heat does not cause much discomfort or produce disease, because of the lack of decaying vegetation and the extreme dryness of the atmosphere. The summer lasts from the latter part of May to the first of October, and during this season rain has seldom been known to fall. During the fall and winter, warm and abundant rains appear in storms of about a week's duration, generally preceded by winds from the south. Snow is seldom seen, except in December or January, when it sometimes appears in a succession of fleecy hoods upon the eastern peaks. Only three times in the last twenty years has snow covered the ground, and then it disappeared in the course of a few hours. There is usually a light frost during December and January, but it does no damage to vegetation even so delicate as the geranium and oleander, which flourish abundantly in the gardens.

A VALUABLE FARM.

THREE miles from Jenny Lind, on the Calaveras River, is one of the most valuable farms of the county, owned by Mansfield F. Gregory, who located there in 1868. This farm is on the river, and will raise anything that can be grown in a temperate clime. The average yield of corn per acre is 40 bushels; barley, 50; wheat, 35; potatoes, 150.

There are 35 acres of fruit, consisting of 2,000 plums and prunes, 400 apples, 200 pears, 150 nectarines, and 1,300 peach trees. In addition to this are 1,000 blackberry vines.

ROBERT GARDNER'S COTTAGE AT COLD SP.

"COLD SPRING RANCH," PROPERTY OF J

WINTER RESIDENCE, ANGELS CAL.

OHN GARDNER, BIG TREE ROAD, CALAVERAS CO.

ELLIOTT, LITH, OAKLAND.

The farm has 600 acres, about 120 of which is rich bottom land, cultivated in orchard, alfalfa, and corn. The remainder is used for stock, which usually consists of 40 head of cattle, 20 hogs, 350 sheep, and 20 horses.

Mansfield F. Gregory was a native of Warwickshire, England, where he was born July 4, 1841. He received a liberal education at some of the best schools in both England and France, where he remained until about seventeen years old, when he came to the United States to join his father, who, owing to financial embarrassments, had left Europe some three years previous, and had settled in Minnesota. Owing to lung difficulties and natural inclination, he kept to a country life, and settled on a farm in St. Croux County, Wisconsin, but the climate there proving too severe, and intensifying the lung troubles, he finally concluded, on the advice of physicians, to try the mild climate of the Pacific Slope, where he has enjoyed excellent health, in fact, during his sixteen years' residence in Calaveras County, he has had to call in the aid of a professional doctor but once.

On first arrival here, he farmed one year on the black lands near Stockton, but sold out and removed to his present farm. He also represents satisfactorily the interests of the Western Fire and Marine Insurance Company of California, in that section of California.

The farm is desirably located, being only five miles from Milton, on the S. and C. Railroad, and nine miles to Wallace, on the new S. J. and S. N. Railroad.

He married Miss A. M. Gibson, in 1862, who was a native of Pittsburg, Pennsylvania. They have four boys and one girl, named: Stockton Mansfield, Wellington Russell, Froane Livingstone, Anna Inez, and Frisby Roy.

A CALAVERAS HOME AND MINE.

THE residence and grounds of Mr. S. S. Moser, represented in this work, are situated at Mokelumne Hill. The place includes four acres of land, which is supplied with an abundance of fruit trees of all the ordinary kinds of fruit grown in that climate. Beautiful shade and ornamental trees also grace the premises, making this one of the prettiest homes in this section.

Mr. S. S. Moser was born in Trumbull County, Ohio, December, 1837. He was a farmer's son, and when twenty-three years old, came to Mokelumne Hill, California, where he has since resided, with the exception of about three months, when he was engaged as teacher, in Amador County. Mr. Moser has followed mining principally, having been strictly confined to that business for the past fifteen years.

The mine in which Mr. Moser is at present interested is a hydraulic mine, called the Bonanza. Mr. Moser owns a half-interest in the property, Mr. S. L. Prindle and Samuel Foorman being the other two proprietors.

This mine is situated about a mile southeast of Mokelumne Hill. The water supply is obtained from the Mokelumne Hill and Campo Seco Ditch and Mining Companies' Ditch.

The mine has been run on the hydraulic system for the past nine years, being a relocation of abandoned mines. A force of from eight to sixteen men are employed, according to the demand occasioned by circumstances. The mine has given good results, being considered the best in the vicinity.

RAISIN INDUSTRY.

[From Calaveras *Prospect*.]

THE vineyardists of Calaveras should turn their attention to the raisin industry. As fine grapes as are grown in any portion of the State are grown on the foot-hill lands of this county. Several years ago a number of farmers in this vicinity planted the raisin grape, but the vines did not receive the proper attention and consequently did not produce well. About a year ago a load of raisin grapes was brought to town from Tuolumne County, where they attend to their orchards and vineyards. The fruit was very large and had an excellent flavor.

The same kind of fruit that is grown in Tuolumne County can be grown in Calaveras with the proper care in planting and cultivating.

"The raisin-making industry," says the Galt *Gazette*, " is slowly but surely increasing, and should continue to increase till it reaches ten times its present proportions. It is one of the industries in which there will be no danger of overproduction for years to come. Every State in the Union is a consumer, and but few localities are producers of this necessary commodity. Among the few localities in which raisin producing is possible, California stands pre-eminently ahead of all, by reason of her climate, which is so well adapted to the growing of the vine and the handling and curing of the fruit.

"While we have to compete with the Eastern States and the whole world in the growing of our present leading product, wheat, these same States and the whole world may be regarded as sure and ready markets for the products of the vine.

"It would therefore seem a wise move on the part of our agriculturists to turn their attention more to an industry in which nature has done so much to make us practically monopolists. The production has increased in the State from about 40,000 boxes ten years ago to 200,000 boxes the present season. The raisin industry has met with great success around Florin and Elk Grove."

BIG TREES OF CALAVERAS.

[Correspondent S. F. *Examiner*.]

WE hitched a couple of farm horses to a spring wagon, filled it with provisions, tents and blankets, and struck out for the mountains, traveling from fifteen to twenty miles per day. The first place we reached of importance was the Big Trees of Calaveras County. I must admit that they staggered my imagination, and exceeded anything in the vegetable growth I had ever seen. In the stump of one of these trees

a ball-room 33 feet across is built, and it requires a ladder of 18 steps to ascend to the top of the log, on which was built a ten-pin alley. It has been burnt up, but the old charred monarch of the forest still remains. Think of it! a hollow log, through which one can ride on horseback 100 feet, and come out through a knot-hole! There are some 90 of these trees, measuring from 50 to 100 feet in circumference, and reaching up to the skies—from 300 to 450 feet.

They are the remnant of a past flora that one time was more common, but are now confined to some dozen groves scattered from here to King's River—grand old trees that have withstood the storms of thousands of winters, and were saplings when Moses was a little boy, found in the bulrushes of the Nile. What a history could they tell! What a monument of growth! Enough to shame the vanity of proud Cheops, the builder of the Pyramids. They have grown and lifted their heads higher and higher, while the proud kingdoms and empires of Egypt, Persia, Greece and Rome have passed away. They lived and flourished when Christ preached repentance to the Jews, and were full-grown trees when our Anglo-Saxon ancestors ran wild in the woods, and painted their faces like the Indians.

From the rings that denote the annual growth of these trees, science has estimated some of them to be 4,000 years old, while they stand over the fallen bodies of a much older growth, covered over with earth and large-growing trees, as it is one of the peculiarities of this timber not to decay. It appears to be a species of redwood.

FINE VINEYARD AND ORCHARD.

ONE of the representative vineyards of this county is that of F. Mayer, near Mokelumne Hill. He purchased the ranch in about 1860. It has now nearly 20 acres in choice vineyard, of about 17,000 vines. The varieties are: Mission, Shassle, Muscat, Zinfandel, Riesling and other varieties. Mr. Mayer manufactures his grapes into wine. Having had much experience in this line, his wine is of excellent quality. He makes white wine, claret, and angelica. He also manufactures brandy. A fine page view of this vineyard, and also orchard, appears in this work. The orchard contains about 600 trees: 25 apple trees, 75 pear trees, 100 peach trees, 50 prunes, 50 plums, 25 apricot, nectarines, almonds, and a few quince trees.

F. Mayer is a native of Germany, which country he left in 1849 for New York, and soon after came to Mokelumne Hill, where he has since remained. By industry, and the application of skilled knowledge, he has obtained a fine property, one of which he has good reason to be proud.

CLEMENTS, SAN JOAQUIN COUNTY, CAL.

THIS thriving village is located on the San Joaquin and Sierra Nevada Narrow Gauge Railroad, twenty miles from Stockton. It derived its name from Thomas Clements, the pioneer farmer, and original founder of the town. Mr. Clements justly deserves the success he is achieving, as the prosperity of the village is mainly due to his enterprising spirit as shown in the erection of good substantial buildings for business purposes.

The Farmers' Trade Union Building is a fine two-story brick, with basement cellar, located in the heart of the village. The building is the finest this side of Stockton, and is well stocked with a choice selection of general merchandise, groceries, provisions, hardware, agricultural implements, etc. Charles Bamert, the manager, is a man in every way qualified for the position he holds. Courteous manners and square dealing have made him a general favorite. The post-office is also kept, with Mr. Bamert as postmaster.

Just east of the Farmers' Trade Union, ground is broken for the erection of a fine brick building, 60x80 feet. N. Townsend will occupy one-half of this with saddlery,

harness, etc. Nathe turns out nothing but first-class work, and those in need of anything in his line will do well to give him a call.

Marceau's Hotel is a good substantial two-story brick building, well furnished. S. Marceau, the proprietor, understands the wants of the traveling public, as his tables and bar are well supplied, and there is no danger of dying of hunger or thirst.

Charles Poppe's Livery and Feed Stable is situated next north of the hotel. Here all kinds of rigs are kept for hire, and horses boarded reasonably. Mr. Poppe contemplates the enlarging of his business by erecting a large and commodious stable.

Clements' Warehouse is located on the railroad, opposite the Farmer's Trade Union. This is a good substantial building, 70x250 feet, managed by Jas. A. Anderson. Here the principal part of the grain is handled that is grown in the surrounding country.

There is a two-story brick blacksmith shop and wagon manufactory, presided over by J. W. Baker, assisted by Jas. T. Jenkins, where all kinds of job work are done with neatness and dispatch. Road carts and wedge cutters are a specialty.

Thomas Clements has just completed a large and magnificent reservoir, or cistern, of about 500,000 gallons capacity. This is situated at about 75 feet altitude above the town and is intended as a water supply for irrigating and fire purposes.

The brick yard is located near by, where all the bricks are manufactured and burned for building purposes.

The streets are properly laid out and planted with shade and ornamental trees, and the town in general presents a scene of activity that impresses the passer-by that energetic men are at the helm, and erelong this little village will have grown to a large town.

Here is located a magnificent public school building where all the facilities of a common education are offered.

One of the leading nurseries in the State

RES. OF M. F. GRERORY. NEAR JENNY LIND, CAL.

RESIDENCE OF J. F. TREAT. SAN ANDREAS, CAL.

"CASA BLANCA", RESIDENCE OF CAPT. H. A. MESSENGER, 2 ½ MILES N.E. OF VALLEY SPRING.

is owned by Jas. A. Anderson. The trees are of the finest growth of any we have ever seen, and the demands for his stock are constantly increasing. This seems to be the home of all kinds of fruits, and erelong we expect to see these foot-hills one continuous orchard.

The Lone Star Mill is a noted landmark, and was erected in 1859, by John Hodges and Judge David S. Terry, and was purchased the following year by Mr. S. L. Magee, the present owner and proprietor. The material used in its construction is granite, procured in the neighborhood. Its capacity is 100 barrels per day. It is supplied with all the modern improvements. The market justifies Mr. Magee in running this mill about nine months during the year.

MOKELUMNE HILL.

THIS is a pretty little place of about 600 inhabitants, lying north of San Andreas, and near the line of Amador County. It has a number of stores and business places. The Calaveras *Chronicle* is published by Messrs. Burce & Day. It is one of the oldest established papers of the State, and is now in its thirty-fourth volume.

Rev. J. B. Fish was the first minister that preached in Mokelumne Hill. He was sent to Sacramento in 1851 by the Methodist Episcopal Conference in the East, and after preaching in that city one year, was sent to Mokelumne Hill in August, 1852. The first church in this place was a tent erected on Church Street, on the lot which is now the site of the residence of Mrs. Guy. The pioneer residents of this place will readily recall to memory the scenes and circumstances of those early times. The first parsonage was located where the Italian garden is now, and was a log cabin owned by a Mr. S. Newman, who generously donated the property to the church.

The first school in Mokelumne Hill was taught in the church tent, by the wife of Mr. Fish, the school numbering five pupils, two white children and three negroes. The daily session of the school was three hours, and the salary of the teacher was $75.00 per month. The pioneer preacher was a gentleman of excellent qualities of heart, charitable and kindly to all, and liked by all who knew him.

One of the oldest and most noted buildings in town is occupied by Mr. Frank W. Peek, a native of Mokelumne Hill, where he was born in 1857. He has always lived at his birthplace. When nineteen years of age he commenced the confectionery business in the Odd Fellows Building. Mr. Peek kept enlarging his business, keeping, besides confectionery, a general variety store. In 1880 he moved to the Hoerchner Building, one of the oldest buildings in town. It is constructed of stone quarried in the vicinity. It has stood the test of fire, resisting the flame when buildings close by were destroyed.

The father of Mr. Peek, Wm. P. Peek, was appointed postmaster in 1877, resigning the present year. The post-office is still kept in the store. Frank W. Peek married Miss May Stedman, a native of San Francisco, in 1880.

GEO. KELTON has a farm of 150 acres, 40 of which are improved, and devoted to hay, fruit, and grain. There are 300 fruit trees, mainly peach, but some apple. There is some stock on the ranch, generally about 25 head of cattle, some hogs and other animals.

Geo. Kelton was born in 1829, in Grafton, New Hampshire, which place he left in 1850 and came to Big Bar, Calaveras County, where he has since principally resided. He married Mrs. M. A. Foss in 1854. They have two boys and two girls.

COPPEROPOLIS.

COPPEROPOLIS, fifteen miles from Milton, is one of the most interesting mining towns extant. The opening of an immense copper mine called it into existence in 1861–62, and here were built the most extensive mining apparatus in the county. At one time there was a population of more than 5,000 inhabitants. At present it is a quiet place, full of deserted houses, with many bright, comfortable homes here and there among them. It has very commodious and well-kept hotels, a beautiful brick Congregational church, and a fine two-story school-house. These two buildings are the best in the county devoted to such purposes. Many of the deserted houses have been moved away, but there remain still the gigantic work sheds, shops, and machine buildings, silent and unfrequented.

The copper ore lies in immense piles of grayish blue stone, glittering from summit to base with crystallized pyrites of the yellow metal, of which there are thousands of tons already above the surface.

At an early period it was a bustling town, and its future was full of bright promise. The population is placed at 150. It has a daily mail and express. It is situated 945 feet above sea level.

One of the early settlers of Copperopolis, was Andrew Fontana, who was born in Rapaoll, Italy, and after a long sea voyage arrived in San Diego in 1849, but soon after came to Calaveras County and engaged in merchandising. He returned to Italy on a pleasure trip, and there married Miss Anunciada Gaziglia, July, 1860, and returned to California. He died in 1884.

The widow is carrying on the business of general merchandising at Copperopolis. She has two good, substantial stores, a dwelling of six rooms, good stock of goods, and is doing a good business; but, owing to the death of her husband, is desirous of selling the business and buildings. (See illustration).

ANGEL'S CAMP AND ALTAVILLE.

THESE places have been for a number of years noted mining towns, and quartz mining is yet extensively and profitably carried on there. Active men are working with a fierce energy at the valuable deposits known to exist in this district, and a good deal of money has been invested in substantial mills.

The principal industry of this section of country is mining, yet its present agricultural resources, which are already vast and far advanced, will increase in extent and value when they are assisted by irrigation. The land is well adapted to vine and fruit raising. These important industries have already become popular with the people, and a great deal of land has recently been taken up and prepared for the growth of the fruit tree and the grape.

The vineyards, the orange, lemon, olive, apricot, prune, peach, apple, pear, gooseberry, blackberry, almond, English walnut, and other orchards, which are so immensely profitable in California, can be cultivated during all the winter. Rolling hills, with deep soil, and covered by a heavy growth of mountain shrubs, indicative of the richness of the earth, bend their winding way for many miles. All this land is of great value for the culture of fruit and grapes, for farming and stock raising. An adequate supply of water will give vitality and fresh vigor to this entire region.

Angel's—the Angel's Camp made famous by the writings of Bret Harte—is about fourteen miles south of San Andreas. It is a pleasant and prosperous place, the streets lined by neat cottages surrounded by small gardens. Here there is a marble-working establishment, and at Altaville, which is really a part of Angel's, being only a mile from it, there is an iron foundry doing a prosperous business. Silk culture has been attempted in Angel's and has met marked success. The *Mountain Echo* is published here by Myron Reed, and is a well-conducted journal.

The foundry, illustrated in our views at Angel's, was erected in 1881 by D. D. Demorest, together with his residence. He has a blacksmith shop in connection with the foundry, but will eventually change this business to another building.

RESIDENCE OF LEO DOLAN, NEAR MURPHYS, CAL.

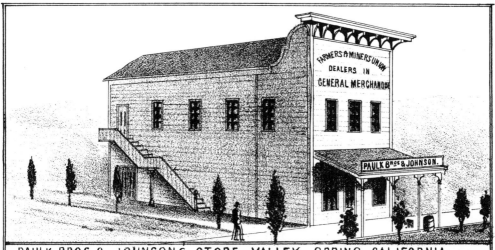

PAULK BROS & JOHNSON'S STORE, VALLEY SPRING, CALIFORNIA.

RESIDENCE OF GEO LATE, VALLEY SPRING, CAL.

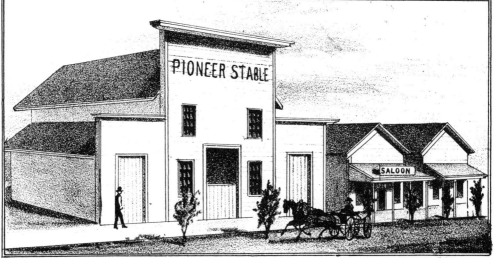

LAMB & COOK'S PIONEER STABLE, HOTEL & SALOON, VALLEY SPRING, CAL.

This foundry is principally engaged in casting shoes and dies for quartz mills, but also does a general jobbing business in both iron and brass. The foundry is run by steam power. Mr. Demorest came to Calaveras County in 1849 and engaged in surface mining until 1860, when he acted as agent of the Union Ditch Company. In 1865 he entered upon proprietorship of the foundry, which he purchased in 1861, which had formerly been run by his brother. He has continued in the foundry business since that date. Mr. Demorest was born in Bergen County, New Jersey, September 15, 1824. He left New York, March 8, 1849, for California, by the Rio Grande route, El Paso, Tucson, and crossing the Colorado River at Fort Yuma.

Snow's is a noted place near Angel's, a view of which is given in this work. The farm consists of 260 acres, producing barley, wheat, and hay. There is an orchard of apples, plums, peaches, nectarines, and grapes, that do well.

James Snow, the owner, is a native of Massachusetts, where he was born in 1830. He started for California in December, 1849, coming by way of Cape Horn, and was 203 days without touching any port, reaching San Francisco in June, 1850. He first tried mining in various localities, with fair success, and afterward turned his attention to farming. He married Miss Margret Kolb in 1860, a native of Germany, and they have six children, named as follows: Margret E., James A., William H., Sophia, Eliza and Robert Snow.

At Angel's, J. C. Scribner keeps a general merchandise store, and a good line of drugs. He also acts as agent for Wells, Fargo & Co.'s express. He came to Calaveras County as early as 1849, and purchased the business formerly conducted by Mr. Angel, the founder of this camp. The wooden building occupied first by Mr. Scribner was burned in 1855, and he replaced it by a very substantial stone building the following year (1856). He has remained in business at this place ever since.

His dwelling is a very substantial one, as may be seen in the view. It is surrounded by a beautiful growth of shade trees and shrubbery, and is a cozy home.

J. C. Scribner was born in Tarrytown, New York, in 1822. His father was a physician. When eighteen years of age he went to New York City, where he engaged as clerk in a grocery establishment. Nine years later, in December, he came to California, going around the Horn, and reaching San Francisco in August, 1849.

He married Mrs. Susan Hogan in 1860, who was a native of England.

CALAVERAS A PROMISING FIELD.

[From the *Rural Press*.]

WE are glad of the opportunity to call attention to the excellencies of Calaveras County, for, though it is a region rich in the history of the mining era of the State, it is too little heard of in the later agricultural period. We regard the county as one of the most promising fields for enterprise and investment and for humble home making.

The county has an area of 622,000 acres, of which it is estimated that there are 300,000 acres of United States Government land subject to entry. Here are found some of the best mines in this State, and the entire county is exceedingly rich in mineral deposits. The baser metals, copper, iron, cinnabar, etc., are found, and ledges of marble, limestone, granite, and undeveloped deposits of coal, are known to exist.

Several most interesting natural wonders are also to be found here, among which are the world renowned Big Trees; the great cave, with its magnificent chambers and wonderful stalactites, and the wonderful bridge also attract the attention and elicit the admiration of tourists from all parts of the world.

Among its other sources of wealth, Calaveras possesses one of the most valuable timber belts in the State, live-oak, sugar and nut-pine predominating. This county is one of the best watered sections of the State, and its undeveloped resources are almost inexhaustible. With the opening which is now made by the new railway, and the rapid extension of orchard and vineyard and poultry farming, the building up of the industries generally of the county may be expected.

LOUISIANA RANCH.

THIS ranch is situated about 4 miles north from Valley Spring, the nearest railroad station. This fine property is owned by Mr. James Megaw, who took up a homestead, a part of the present ranch, in 1873. In 1877 he purchased 320 acres of land adjoining his homestead, of which he has since sold 40 acres; but during the present year (1885) has purchased another place of 80 acres also adjoining the homestead, which now gives an aggregate of 520 acres to the ranch.

Besides this place, Mr. Megaw has a mountain ranch of 160 acres, situated 40 miles east of the home ranch, on a branch of the Mokelumne River.

Mr. Megaw gives his main attention to dairying, having 45 milch cows, from which large quantities of fine butter are produced. He has also 65 head of young stock. Mr. Megaw will drive his stock, in-

STAGE DRIVING THROUGH A BIG TREE.

RESIDENCE OF THOS MC CARTY, 4 MILES WEST OF COPPEROPOLIS, CAL.

ELLIOTT LITH. OAKLAND.

RES. & STORE OF W.H. CASE, COPPEROPOLIS.   "MILTON HOTEL", J.C. BUNDS. PROP. (FOR SALE)

RESIDENCE OF J.M. BAKER, COPPEROPOLIS,

RESIDENCE & STORE OF MRS. A. FONTANA. COPPEROPOLIS, CAL.

cluding his dairy, to the mountain ranch the present season, where he will continue the manufacture of butter.

The buildings at the Louisiana Ranch are numerous and substantial. The dwelling is a painted structure of nine rooms, surrounded by a luxuriant growth of fruit and ornamental trees and shrubbery, making a very pleasant home. The out-buildings consist of a cow barn, horse barn, a large hay barn, wagon barn, and granary and store house, 2 cow sheds, 3 hog sheds, and 7 poultry houses. There is a fine old orchard on the place of about 150 apple trees, besides an abundance of apricot, pear, fig, plum and peach trees. There is also a fine old vineyard containing about 1 200 vines.

The ranch is very abundantly supplied with water from seven never-failing springs, and by the Mokelumne Ditch, which runs for a distance of one and a half miles through it.

Mr. Megaw and his industrious family have been indefatigable in their labors on their home to improve it, and their efforts have met with satisfactory results.

James Megaw was born May 28, 1829, near Newville, Cumberland County, Pennsylvania. He was raised on a farm, and remained at home until 22 years of age, when he went to Dayton, Ohio, where he remained until March, 1854. At this time he started overland for California, stopping at Independence, Missouri, whence he departed in May, reaching Volcano, Amador County, the following August. At this place he engaged in mining. From this time until 1880, he continued in the business. In 1876, while in Placerville, Eldorado County, he was united in marriage to Mrs. Mary Shira, also a native of Pennsylvania. On account of the loss of health, occasioned by his occupation in chloride works, Mr. Megaw was obliged to give up mining, and has since given his whole attention to farming.

FARMING IN CALAVERAS.

[From Calaveras *Chronicle*.]

THROUGHOUT the central portion of the county, where placer mining was most extensively pursued in early days, there is quite a large area of arable land. The inclinations of many of the rolling hills, or offshoots, of the Sierra Nevada Mountains, are so gradual as to permit the husbandman to till them without difficulty, and the many cozy, well-sheltered little valleys bordering upon the mountain streams, are among the most inviting and productive lands in the State. Time and experiments will reveal the fact that these lands immediately below the snow belt are infinitely adapted to fruit culture, more particularly the apple, pear, and grape, than the valley. A great future undoubtedly awaits that region in the development of the agricultural and horticultural capabilities of the situation.

That fruits attain rare perfection on these mountain terraces and in the little valleys nestling close to the flanks of the rugged, snow-clad mountains, which nature has provided as a great reservoir to hold back abundance of water until it is needed to alleviate the thirst of the arid soil, has already been demonstrated. The produce of the plains in the way of table grapes and wine, is greatly inferior to that of the higher lands. The quality of the pears produced on the red soil along the limestone range, extending in a northerly direction through the county, is very superior; and as for sound, fully and finely developed, finely flavored apples, Californians will have to procure them from mountain orchards if they obtain a home product of the first quality at all.

The present industrial prospects of the county are brighter and of a more encouraging character than they have been for many years past. There has been during the past year an extraordinary inquiry for mountain lands. Astonishing as it may appear, the poorest foot-hill land in the county—the district immediately west of the auriferous belt extending from the Stanislaus River, on the south, to the Calaveras River, on the north—is now sought for with avidity. A large share of these lands can be irrigated from the canals constructed to convey water to the miners in early days. Twelve years ago there were about 48,000 acres of lands inclosed by fences; now there is four times that area fenced, and many quarter-sections homesteaded and pre-empted, the lines of which are only marked by the surveyor's stakes.

MOKELUMNE AND CAMPO SECO CANAL AND MINING COMPANY.

THE works of this company were begun in 1852, and completed to Mokelumne Hill in 1853, with a capacity of carrying 1,000 inches of water, miner's measure, and subsequently extended to Campo Seco, Comanche, and vicinities, a distance of 60 miles from the dam at the head of the canal.

The object of the enterprise was for the purpose of supplying water in washing out gold from the auriferous earth of this rich mineral region.

Like all enterprises of this character begun at an early day of our mining industry, the vicissitudes of the undertaking have been many, owing to inexperience of projectors in works of this kind, and the high price of labor and material during the construction.

But these difficulties have all been successfully overcome, and the company is now in a position to materially assist in the development of this section of the county in its mineral and agricultural wealth.

The works were originally constructed by building a wooden flume laid on the ground and carried across depressions on high tressel work. Owing to the enormous expense of repairs through the rapid decay of wooden structures, caused by the extremes of heat and cold, dry and wet, this has been changed by the substitution of gravel ditch and iron pipes.

This line of ditch has the prior right to the water of the South Fork and the Middle Fork of the Mokelumne River, streams fed by melting snow in summer, therefore always supplied with water.

The ditch system consists of a large storage reservoir in the mountains, distributing reservoirs where needed. A line of ditch, and branches, extends through Mokelumne Hill, supplying this place with water for town use, also Campo Seco, and Comanche, as leading points, besides Grain Mine, Pine Peak, Central Hill, Chilo Camp, Poverty Ridge, and Cat Camp, and intermediate places, enabling residents along the line to wash either quartz or placer mines, to cultivate the soil successfully by irrigation, or to run machinery by having the necessary power brought to their doors.

In the building of the San Joaquin and Sierra Nevada Narrow Gauge Railroad through this section, the advantages and worth of this system of water supply will become more conspicuous and appreciated, as the agriculturist will have a ready means of transportation to market of his products, raised by successful irrigation of his trees, vines, and other crops, almost independent of the seasons.

The new stations of Valley Springs and Burson are within a short distance of this line of canal, and connections are now being made by which the surrounding region can be supplied with water for any purpose desired, but principally irrigation.

We give an illustration of a section of the canal at Mokelumne Hill, town reservoir, and office, residence, and out-buildings.

SAN ANDREAS, THE COUNTY SEAT.

SAN ANDREAS is situated centrally as to population. It was formerly a mining center, but now is a quiet, pleasant little place, the principal business clustering about the Court House and the neigh-

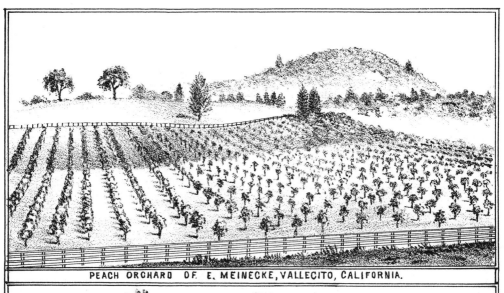

PEACH ORCHARD OF. E. MEINECKE, VALLECITO, CALIFORNIA.

"WALNUT GROVE," RESIDENCE OF MRS. CATHERINE BATTEN, NEAR VALLECITO.

THE RESIDENCE OF JAMES SNOW HAWKEYE NEAR ANGELS.

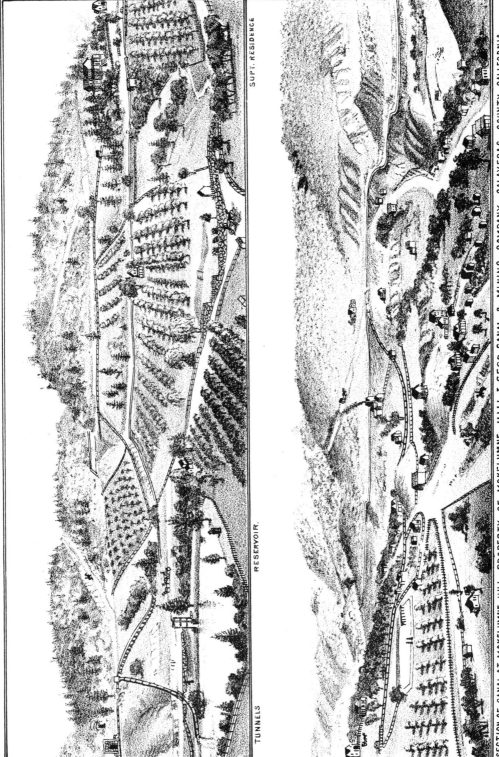

SUPT. RESIDENCE.

RESERVOIR.

TUNNELS

SECTION OF CANAL AT MOKELUMNE HILL, PROPERTY OF MOKELUMNE HILL & SECO CANAL & MINING COMPANY, CALAVERAS COUNTY, CALIFORNIA.

boring ranches. The County Hospital is situated here, but has few occupants. It depends mainly upon its lodes for support, yet fruit-growing and stock-raising are important factors in the nourishment imparted to her growth. The altitude is 1,600 feet.

There are here two prosperous weekly newspapers, the *Calaveras Citizen*, established in 1870, and now published by C. R. Beal, and the *Calaveras Prospect*, now in its fourth volume, and published by Gitchell & Salcido.

The first paper issued in Calaveras County was the *Independent*, on Wednesday, September 24, 1856, by George Armor. In speaking of San Andreas, it says: "All places have had a beginning, and so had San Andreas. In the winter of 1848, a few Mexicans encamped at the forks of the gulch (since called San Andreas), about one-fourth of a mile above where the town now stands, and commenced working in the bed of the gulch by sinking holes, and washing out with "batteas." In the fall of 1849 their number considerably increased, but the place was not looked upon as worthy of any great note as a mining locality. But in the winter of 1849, or spring of 1850, a few Americans came in and commenced operations in the main gulch, which soon had a tendency to bring in others.

In the meantime the Spanish population continued to increase, until, in the fall and winter of 1850, they numbered 1,200 or 1,500. At this time the principal part were encamped on the hill-side, on which is now located the town of San Andreas, and on all sides were seen small tents, such as usually designated any important mining locality in the palmy, prosperous days of 1849–50. The mines were rich, every person was doing well, and of course gambling shops and fandango houses were in full blast, and dark and desperate deeds were committed.

In the spring of 1851 was erected the "Bella Union," the first frame building in San Andreas, which answered the purpose of court room, drinking saloon, gambling house, and dance house. About the time of its completion, rich diggings were discovered at Mokelumne Hill. A rush was made, everybody followed the rush, and San Andreas became nearly depopulated.

Early in the summer of 1851, Capt. Robert Pope came to this place, located the right of way, and surveyed the route of a ditch leading from Willow Creek to the foothills north of San Andreas. Shortly afterwards a company, calling themselves the Miner's Ditch Company, commenced a ditch along the same route, which was completed and water running through early in the spring of 1852. A suit was begun between Captain Pope and the Mining Company, which, in 1853, was decided in Pope's favor. In the fall of 1851, the miners began to return from the stampede they had taken in the direction of Mokelumne Hill, and the following winter San Andreas became again quite a flourishing camp. During the winter of 1851 another ditch company was formed, called the Union Company, for the purpose of bringing water from Murray's Creek. This was completed in 1852.

In the spring of 1852, the diggings on Gold Hill were discovered. During the years 1853 and 1854 the town made but small progress in the way of improvement, but in the spring and summer of 1855 it took a fresh start. That year, Kohlburg & Co. built the first stone house. The American Restaurant and Thomas Corcoran's, both stone buildings, were erected that year. In the winter of 1856 a fire swept away a good portion of the town, including the Bella Union, the first house built in town.

In 1856 the Odd Fellows' Building was built. It is of brick, with stone basement, two stories high, 30 feet above the basement, 50 by 30 feet, costing $8,000.

San Andreas can boast of one of the finest livery establishments outside of the cities that there is in the State. It is owned and managed by Mr. J. F. Washburn, and is complete in every particular. His arrangements are such that he can supply on short notice

MORANS RANCH, 12 MILES N.E. OF MURPHYS CALAVERAS CO. CAL.
PROPERTY OF JOHN & MICHAEL MORAN.

RESIDENCE OF D.D. DEMOREST. ALTAVILLE CAL.

carriages and conveyances for any number of tourists, who may desire to visit any points of interest. The completion of the S. J. and S. N. Railroad to this place makes this now a favorite route of travel to the Big Trees and Yosemite. Correspondence is solicited, and all communications promptly answered. Carriages, buggies, and saddle horses, as well as suitable vehicles for commercial travelers, are furnished on short notice, and on reasonable terms.

The Metropolitan Hotel is located in San Andreas, and is the leading hotel of the county, and acknowledged by all travelers to be excellently managed and in all respects a first-class house. It was purchased by B. F. Hawes in 1879. He was a native of Kentucky, where he was born in 1830. When twenty-two years old he came to California overland to Placerville. He came to Calaveras County in 1852 and engaged in mining, and also in Placerville and Murphy's. At Campo Seco he mined twenty-two years, from 1853 to 1875, and is still interested in mining having a third ownership in the Campo Seco Copper Mine.

In 1875 he was elected Sheriff of Calaveras County, which office he held until 1880.

He married Miss Mildred E. Syme in 1859, who was a native of Arkansas. Names of children living are: Frank T., Talton, Harry, Virginia L., Annie, and Eva Hawes.

PHOENIX LIVERY STABLE, at San Andreas, is managed by P. Masterson, who makes a specialty of fitting out parties for the Big Trees or Yosemite or other resorts. Parties going to the mountains, Big Trees and Yosemite Falls, wishing teams, can be furnished with driver if desired, also suitable vehicles for drummers with large trunks. Carriages, buggies, wagons, and saddle horses for hire on reasonable terms. All telegrams answered free of cost. Address: P. Masterson, San Andreas.

AMONG the prominent merchants of San Andreas is Chancey R. Lloyd, who owns the brick building illustrated elsewhere. He has a fine trade, and keeps a general stock of merchandise. He settled at San Andreas about the year 1865, and opened a store where the express office is now kept. About the year 1875 he opened the store now occupied by him.

C. R. Lloyd is a native of Bradford County, Pennsylvania. When fourteen years of age he started out in the peddling business, which he followed until 1855, when he came to California—came across with cattle train. On the way, at Black Hills, the trains were attacked by Indians, only one of the party being wounded. He arrived at Placerville, then Hangtown, and still followed the vocation of peddling with good success, thus fitting himself for a good merchant at a later date.

"CASA BLANCA."

THIS house was named Casa Blanca, or White House, after a celebrated house in Arizona, formerly situated on the Lenoita below old Fort Buchanan, where Captain H. A. Messenger was frequently during his service in the army. It is beautifully situated two and one-half miles from the new town of Valley Spring, at the head of a beautiful valley, and is the favorite resort of those who like an even temperature. Plenty of good water and beautiful shade and vine all around the house and garden. Captain Messenger was one of the original projectors of the San Joaquin and Sierra Nevada Railroad, and has taken a deep interest in its welfare, as well as assisting to the full extent of his means in grading the road, he being the present contractor for that work. Those desiring home comforts and all the luxuries of a quiet home life and fresh fruit, should not fail to give him a call, and try the accommodations at "Casa Blanca."

Captain Hiram Ashley Messenger was born in Peru, Berkshire County, Massachusetts. He left there April 19, 1852, and, crossing the mountains and plains, arrived in Stockton, October 10th, and from here went to Mokelumne Hill.

In 1860, he discovered the copper mines near Campo Seco, and did well there until 1864, when he sold out.

He raised a company of volunteers and went with them as captain to Arizona, and was mustered out of service in 1866. Mr. Messenger ably represented his constituents in the Legislature one term.

His farm is one of the best in that locality, consisting of 1,100 acres, of which 35 acres is rich bottom land and the balance good grazing, producing wheat, barley, alfalfa, and other crops. In the orchard are 100 peach, 50 apple, 20 apricot, 20 plum, and orange and olive trees, also a good variety of small fruits.

He married Miss Hattie L. Wilkins in 1859, who was a native of New Hampshire. They have children named Nelson O., Mary F., Maud W., Hiram H., and Hattie May Messenger.

VALLEY SPRINGS.

THIS flourishing new town is growing rapidly. It is situated on the San Joaquin and Sierra Nevada Railroad, and a more beautiful, as well as favorable location for a village could not have been selected. The town has been well planned throughout. The streets are all named, and the work of grading them will commence immediately. The streets are all wide and regular.

Building lots are selling at a good figure, commanding a variety of prices according to location.

Every block has a row of trees around it that will make the town a mass of beautiful foliage as soon as they are grown. The water has been turned into the reservoir and the connection made with pipes so that the town is now supplied with water through them.

From the outset it was the intention of the management to make Valley Springs a desirable point of resort, for people who seek a healthy foot-hill climate and a desirable location accessible by rail. In point of beauty, scenery, climate, healthfulness, and hotel accommodations, the new town will rank second to none in the mountains. It is backed by a good country, and is the distributing point for all parts of the county, and being connected by rail with Stockton, Sacramento, and San Francisco, will naturally become a busy business center. This alone suffices to mark its importance and give it a prestige.

Messrs. Paulk Bros. & Johnson have erected a large store for general merchandise, which is one of the best buildings in the county. A view of it will be found in our illustration of Valley Springs. This firm have a fine and varied assortment of goods, and are also engaged in real estate and insurance. If any of our readers are inclined to locate in a fine climate where all kinds of fruit—grapes and oranges—grow, we advise them to call on this firm and let them show what is done on the foot-hill farms of Calaveras.

Messrs. Lamb & Cook have erected the "Pioneer Livery Stable," which has been sketched, and appears in the illustrations of Valley Springs. They have also built a restaurant and dwelling house, and, adjoining this, a saloon.

The railroad company have laid out eighteen blocks, each surrounded with walnut trees from one to two years old, and all boxed in good style. Every tree has a tube leading from above the surface of the ground to its roots, whereby they are irrigated without baking the ground or scalding the bark, as might be the case during the summer months. The same company are also grading the streets as fast as practicable.

GEO. LATE is a pioneer of California, having arrived in San Francisco, August 22, 1849, after a trip around Cape Horn on the bark *Kirkland*. Mr. Late has been engaged in mining like all early comers, but now resides near Valley Springs, where he is engaged in farming and raising cattle. He has always resided in Calaveras County since coming to California, and is well known and identified with the interests of his section and county.

He took a trip East in 1853, and married

"LOUISIANA RANCH" REAR VIEW – PROPERTY OF JAMES MEGAW, 4 MILES FROM VALLEY SPRINGS, CAL.

ELLIOT P. OAK CAL.

"LOUISIANA RANCH," FRONT VIEW, RESIDENCE & FARM BUILDINGS OF JAMES MEGAW.

DURHAM BULL "DUKE"

Rebecca C. Shafer. They embarked for California the 22d of June, 1854, by way of the Panama Route, and arrived in San Francisco July 24th. He was married February 28, 1854, and they have five boys and one girl.

MILTON.

THIS is a post, express, and telegraph office. It is the terminus of the Stockton and Copperopolis Division of the Central Pacific Railroad, twenty-eight miles from Stockton, and where connections with the stage line for the Yosemite, Big Trees, and mountain resorts generally is made.

Milton Hotel is kept by J. C. Bund, and travelers will find it a desirable stopping place. Mr. Bund came to California in April, 1853, from Missouri, and settled first in San Joaquin County, and engaged in merchandising, and afterward came to Milton.

VALLECITO FLAT DESCRIBED.

VALLECITO FLAT, which has often been the theme of scientific writers, is a basin, or depression, the lower portion of which when opened by a tunnel will be a natural outlet for the whole surrounding country. It has an average width of from two hundred to fifteen hundred feet; is from sixty to two hundred feet in depth, and extends in a northerly and easterly direction from the place of beginning for a distance of some three miles or more. In many places where it has been worked, the blue gravel part was found to be from fifteen to thirty feet in thickness, and very rich, having often paid as high as fifteen dollars per cubic yard.

Vallecito Flat has long ago engaged the attention of ambitious men. Its rich deposits have brought to its walls an army of toilers who have returned to their homes with the recompense of abundant gold. Practical mining has attested the wonderful richness of this region, and science has attempted to measure its extent, while the annals of California record its marvelous resources.

Edward Meinecke has one of the most valuable orchards of this section. Our artist has given a sketch of it, showing its location and surroundings. It is the largest and best peach orchard in the county, containing over 3,000 choice trees that produce large crops of luscious peaches. The residence of Mr. Meinecke does not appear in this view.

Among the early settlers of this locality was John Batten, born in Wales, in 1820, and came to Pennsylvania when nineteen years of age, and from there came to California in February, 1852. He engaged in mining in Tuolumne County for a while, but soon bought a farm of 160 acres, mostly level land, producing large crops of wheat and barley. There is a good orchard of 100 apple, 500 peach, 500 plum, 100 pear, and 100 walnut trees.

Mr. Batten married Miss Catherine Reese, in 1850. They have children, named as follows: Thomas, George, Fred, John W., David, and Sarah Batten.

John Batten died October 11, 1882. Since this time mining property owned by him has been involved in litigation between Mrs. Sarah Mitchell, the daughter, and her mother, Catherine Batten. Said litigation involves property to the amount of a number of thousand dollars; 320 acres of land is in the mining claim of Bowling Green, and Dashaway. The property now held by Catherine Batten amounts to 240 acres of land.

WHAT A PIONEER SAYS.

DAVID B. NYE has a fruit, pasture, and vineyard farm of 160 acres. He came from Falmouth, Massachusetts, around Cape Horn, reaching San Francisco February 18, 1849. He says: "I came to this county in March, 1850, and have resided here continuously, with the exception of three years, from 1868–71, in which time there has been many changes and reverses, but at this late day the light of prosperity begins to shine upon the old pioneers, and we soon will see better days, as soon the iron horse will traverse the entire length of our county, and cause the once thriving mining towns—but now dead—to assume a new feature in the way of pleasant homes, and surrounded with all the luxuries of life, as no locality can surpass this county for climate and abundance of good fruit. It is the poor man's paradise. Soon we will hear the locomotive of the S. J. & S. N. Railroad at the new town of Valley Springs, two and a half miles distant. In writing up your description of this county, too much praise cannot be said in regard to homes for those who want happiness and prosperity, as there is room for thousands to settle and to prosper.

TELEGRAPH CITY.

THIS place consists chiefly of the residence and farm of Edward Parks, who was born in South Carolina, in February, 1822. He was a veteran in the Mexican War. He came to California by way of Panama, where he remained nine months in business, and reached San Francisco in 1851.

He is now quite an extensive farmer, having 1,000 acres of grazing land, where he keeps about 70 head of cattle, 70 hogs, and 10 mules and other stock.

He married Mrs. Breckenridge, May 1, 1856, who was a native of Scotland. They have four children: Robert B., Lucy, Mary, and Ella Parks.

SUCCESSFUL FRUIT ORCHARD.

ANSIL DAVIS has a successful fruit place of 40 acres at Douglas Flat. He was a native of Maine, and came to Calaveras County in 1861.

The southern, or foot-hill, section of Calaveras is peculiarly adapted to the production of every description of fruit, as is attested by the innumerable vineyards and orchards in luxuriant growth throughout that portion of the county.

Among them we particularly notice that of Mr. Davis, who has 3,000 trees of all varieties of fruit. The orchard bears abundantly, and the fruit is of superior flavor. Apples, pears, plums, and peaches grow to perfection, and some of the finest varieties have been cultivated. He also has 3,000 grape vines of selected varieties. Grapes have only lately received attention in this county, but that they are doing as well here as in any of the other mountain counties of the State, is easily seen, for a small acreage was put out to these products as many as twenty years ago and have produced well ever since.

The reader is referred to one of our largest illustrations, representing the home, farm, and surroundings of Mr. Davis, as it gives to the Eastern reader a very good idea of a foot-hill fruit farm. The hills are in some places very rugged and rocky, while the soil of the valleys is a kind of reddish clayey-sandy soil, and the side-hills are more or less reddish and sandy, and covered with grease brush, chemissal, nut pines, and scrub oaks, the leaves of which have fallen to the ground and decayed year after year, enriching and fertilizing the soil.

DUNBAR'S RANCH.

THE Dunbar Ranch is situated on the road leading from Murphy's to the Calaveras Big Trees, about eleven miles from Murphy's and about four miles from the Trees. The altitude is about 3,500 feet above the sea level, and the situation for healthfulness and salubrity of climate cannot be surpassed.

About 100 acres are situated in a long narrow valley, about 200 feet below the surrounding hills, and have a deep, rich, black soil of inexhaustible richness, being from 3 to 5 feet in depth, and produces abundant crops of timothy hay and potatoes.

Other crops could doubtless be grown, but

T.J. MATTESON'S STAGE. APPROACHING THE BIG TREES.

R. SENTER & CO. GENERAL MERCHANDISE STORE. MURPHYS, CAL.

RESIDENCE OF S.S. MOSER. MOKELUMNE HILL.

heretofore these have been the leading ones produced.

The more hardy kinds of fruit, especially apples, could be produced in unlimited quantities. This valley land, save for a few straggling oaks, is clear from timber, and presents a beautiful contrast to the surrounding hill-sides, which rise on every side covered with a heavy growth of magnificent pines.

Standing in primeval grandeur, unculled by the hand of the despoiler, the giant sugar and yellow pines reach often to a height of 200 to 250 feet, and have a well maintained diameter of from 2 to 6 feet. The most moderate estimates place the whole amount of timber on the tract at from 12,000,000 to 15,000,000 feet.

The whole property consists of 880 acres of land all covered with United States patents, and is doubtless one of the finest locations for lumber business on this slope of the Sierras.

All over this tract are abundant springs of crystal clear water, making the ground sufficiently moist so that all crops grow without irrigation, and adapting it equally well for dairying purposes.

Mr. Freeman Dunbar, the father of the present owner, is a pioneer of California, coming to the State from New Hampshire in 1850, and was for many years extensively engaged in lumbering. Mr. Willis Dunbar, the owner of the ranch, was born in Sullivan County, New Hampshire, in 1838, and came to California in 1856, remaining till 1866, when he returned to his native State, attending the Manchester Business College, from which institution he graduated in 1867.

After an extended trip through the South and West, he returned to California, and assumed charge of his father's extensive lumber operations for several years. In 1878 he had charge of settling the large estate of Mr. Kimball, one of the largest owners in the Union Water Company.

Soon afterward he became Superintendent of the Union Water Company, which position he still holds.

MITCHLER'S HOTEL.

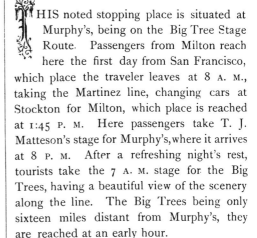 HIS noted stopping place is situated at Murphy's, being on the Big Tree Stage Route. Passengers from Milton reach here the first day from San Francisco, which place the traveler leaves at 8 A. M., taking the Martinez line, changing cars at Stockton for Milton, which place is reached at 1:45 P. M. Here passengers take T. J. Matteson's stage for Murphy's, where it arrives at 8 P. M. After a refreshing night's rest, tourists take the 7 A. M. stage for the Big Trees, having a beautiful view of the scenery along the line. The Big Trees being only sixteen miles distant from Murphy's, they are reached at an early hour.

The Mitchler Hotel is among the best of the country. The building was built by J. L. Sperry and John Perry, in 1855. In 1859 it was burned, the rear portion being constructed of wood. It was immediately rebuilt by the owners, the entire building being of stone, making it fire-proof. In September, 1882, Mr. Mitchler and his mother purchased the hotel. In 1884 Mr. Mitchler's brother, Frank A., also bought an interest, the partnership now being Mrs. Elizabeth Mitchler & Sons.

C. P. Mitchler was born in 1859, at Murphy's, and has always resided there.

Mr. Frank A. Mitchler was born at Murphy's, California, November 8, 1863. He has resided in Murphy during life.

Mrs. Elizabeth Mitchler's maiden name was Elizabeth Angels, and she was married in Bavaria, in 1847, to Jacob Cline. With him she came to America in 1851. They remained in New York a few months, from whence they removed to San Francisco. They remained there but a short time, when they returned to Tuolumne County. Here Mr. Cline engaged in the bakery business. Mrs. Cline obtained a divorce, in 1856, from Mr. Cline, and married Mr. George Mitchler, at Murphy's, in 1858. He died in 1866. His death was tragic, being at the hands of a Mexican, in Mariposa County. The assassination was occasioned from jealousy growing out of misunderstanding in regard to mining property in which Mr. Mitchler was interested   The murderer met his death in the same manner shortly after.   Mrs. Mitchler's children by her second husband are the brothers already mentioned and a daughter, E. Adelena, now Mrs. George Scantlebury, of Murphy's, California.

BEAUTIFULLY LOCATED RANCH.

ABOUT 12 miles northeast of Murphy's, and 3 miles from the Big Trees, is the ranch of John Moran, consisting of 1,100 acres, 100 of which are improved and the balance is fine timber, consisting of sugar pine, yellow pine, fir and oak.   The timber completely surrounds the improved land, which produces excellent potatoes and vegetables generally.   There are a few apple, plum, and other fruit trees.   There are generally on the place 30 head of cattle, besides hogs, sheep and other animals.

John Moran was a native of Ross Common, Ireland, and came to New York in 1847, and engaged in ship building.   He left February, 1852, and reached Murphy's in April, 1852, and engaged in mining until 1864, and purchased his ranch in 1870.   He married Miss Theresa Curren in 1861.   They have two children, Katie and Thomas.

Mr. Michael Moran, brother to John, is also interested in the ranch property.   He came from New York in 1857 and also engaged in mining.   He resides in the place the entire year.   Mr. Michael Moran married Elizabeth Flannigan in 1849.

FINE RESIDENCE AND RESORT.

THE large residence and grounds illustrated elsewhere of Captain Thomas B. Meader are very pleasantly located at Copperopolis.   There is connected with the farm an orchard with a variety of fruits and grapes.   It is quite a resort during the summer time.   The large mansion has very pleasant verandas surrounding three sides, from which fine views of the surrounding country are obtained.

The proprietor, Thomas B. Meader, was a native of Nantucket, Massachusetts, where he was born in September, 1815.   His early life for about twenty years before coming to California was spent on the sea.   In April, 1849, he set out for California from New Bedford in the ship *Mayflower*, Captain George Randall, and reached San Francisco in September, 1849.   He mined at Mormon Island thirty miles above Sacramento on the American River.   He came to Calaveras County in 1864 and engaged in copper mining at Copperopolis.   He married Miss Susan E. Hatch in March, 1840.   She was a native of Falmouth, Massachusetts.

A COMFORTABLE HOME.

ONE of the model homes of Calaveras is that of S. A. Perry, at Douglass Flat.   He has a comfortable home, with a nice orchard of apple, plum, fig, cherry, and apricot trees, and a garden where all kinds of vegetables are raised.   He also has five cows, several head of young cattle, sheep, horses, and poultry, on his place.   S. A. Perry & Sons are engaged in general merchandising at Douglass Flat, and do quite an extensive business.   He is postmaster; two of the sons are of the firm.

Stephen Addison Perry was born in Plainfield, Vermont.   His father died when he was fourteen years old.   After attending school part of two years he began merchandising, and after a few years removed to Boston.   The wonderful stories of gold in California soon induced him to start for this then far off land in 1849, on a steamer bound for the Isthmus.   After delays and adventures on the Isthmus, he sailed on the steamer *Unicorn*, and arrived in San Francisco February 5, 1850.   He went immediately to the mines,

CAMPING IN CALAVERAS COUNTY.

and worked for about two years. He was married on the 21st of February, 1853, having sent for the lady to whom he was engaged. She came on steamer around Cape Horn. He then permanently located at Douglass Flat. They have a family of four children. The only daughter has been a very successful teacher, having a life diploma. The sons are all in active business employments.

COLD SPRING RANCH.

THE timbered section of Calaveras County contains not only the largest trees in the world, but also extensive tracts of the largest and most valuable of California pine. Visitors to this section are surprised and delighted with the magnificence of these forests. Some experienced travelers even declare views which present themselves from various commanding points to be superior to any similar scene with which they are acquainted. In the midst of one of the noblest sections of this timber belt is situated the "Cold Spring Ranch." To reach the ranch it is necessary to travel either by the San Joaquin and Sierra Nevada Railroad, which connects at Lodi with the Central Pacific, and traveling to its terminus at Valley Springs, where connection is made with stage, or the more popular route by the way of Stockton, connecting with the Milton Branch, which connects at Milton with T. J. Matteson's excellently managed stage line, whence the tourist is conveyed to this mountain resort, which is situated two and one-half miles above the Calaveras Big Trees on the Big Tree and Carson Valley Toll Road. When purchased by the owner, Mr. John Gardner, of Judge Hall, of Vallicito, California, it contained 320 acres, which have been increased by subsequent purchases until it reaches double that amount—an entire section.

The altitude of this ranch, about 4,800 feet, is too great for the production of many crops raised in the valleys, but makes it excellent grass and grazing land. The chief value of the ranch, however, is in its timber and its utility as a summer resort, and trading depot for herders and stock men who inhabit the mountains a goodly portion of the time. An excellent business is transacted with this class. The buildings on the place are substantial and commodious, the large two and a half story hotel being especially noticeable. The facilities for accommodating guests are so excellent that Mr. Gardner has had considerable patronage from tourists who find this such a charming resort. Opportunities are abundant for their enjoyment, hunting in the forests, or fishing in the San Antone, a splendid stream, running through the place, well stocked with trout, being among the most popular amusements. Mr. Gardner adds shake-making to his other industries, being the most extensive dealer in this class of building material in that section.

John Gardner was born at Paisley, West Scotland, in 1822. When twelve years of age he learned the dyer's trade, which he followed until 1840, when he learned the lath-splitting trade, which occupied his attention until 1849, when he emigrated to America, locating in New York City, where he again followed the dyeing business. In 1851 he came to California by the Cape Horn route, being five months on the voyage. For two years he remained in San Francisco, where he was variously occupied, until he went to Angel's Camp, Calaveras County, when he engaged in mining, which he followed fourteen years. In 1866 he purchased the Cold Spring Ranch, where he resides during the summer, returning to his residence at Angel's to spend the winter. Mr. Gardner was married in Scotland, in 1844, to Miss Rebecca Dorrington, a native of Greenock. She accompanied her husband to New York, but he preceded her to California. Mrs. Gardner followed by the Isthmus route six months later. The remainder of the family consists of a daughter, Elizabeth, now Mrs. H. S. Blood, of Angel's, and two sons, Robert and George.

CUTLER'S VALUABLE FARM.

AT Jenny Lind, on the banks of the Calaveras River, is the valuable farm of W. O. Cutler. This place is represented by one of our largest illustrations. In the rear of the large and commodious residence will be noticed the Calaveras River winding among the trees, on the bank of which is the farm of Mr. Cutler. He has in the foreground fields of cultivated land, while, nearer the house, are the orchard and vineyard. This farm is considered one of the finest river farms in the county, producing in abundance both fruit and grain and stock.

ORANGES IN CALAVERAS.

(From Solano Republican.)

A NUMBER of old settlers put out some orange, citron and lemon trees. One man set out a few oranges and citrons twenty-four years ago, almost in the town of Campo Seco. The oranges this year are large and luscious as any we ever saw, while the citrons, being those of commerce, are quite a curiosity, very few people in this county having ever seen them green or growing. He set out a large acreage of oranges about seven years ago, and they are just now coming into full bearing.

Geo. W. Cutter bought this place about five years ago, and he informs us that one year they gathered from one of the older trees 2,000 oranges, and that from three of the oldest 900 were gathered in one day, and it was impossible to tell, on account of the enormous quantity still remaining on the trees, that any fruit had been taken off. This year the fruit has been injured some by the high winds which blew the fruit against the tree, bruising it some and causing it to rot.

Among our illustrations will be found a sketch of this place.

Wherever Calaveras oranges have been exhibited, they are pronounced of a superior quality. There can be no doubt of their successful cultivation in the warm valleys of Calaveras.

Figs also do extremely well, and Calaveras can boast of the largest fig trees in the State.

BEAUTIFUL VALLEY FARM.

LEO DOLAN, near Murphy's, has a fine valley farm, beautifully located, as may be seen by the illustration. It is well fenced and supplied with out-buildings. In the rear, toward the hills, is the orchard, and another to the east. In front of the house is a little lake affording water for stock as well as recreation. It is supplied by one of the largest springs in the county. There are two of these very large springs of beautiful water on the farm. They supply an abundance of water for irrigation, stock and reservoir, thus adding largely to the value of the place.

CAMPO SECO.

THIS is one of the old settled points in the county. Among the prominent residents there is James Creighton, who was born in Ohio, August 17, 1832. He arrived in California and engaged in mining at Volcano and other places, with moderate success. In 1860 he engaged in the business of butchering. He has a farm of 320 acres devoted to grazing. He keeps about 150 head of cattle. He married Miss Ham, February 14, 1856, who was a native of Illinois. They have four children: Ada Louise, Sarah E., Hattie E., and Laura B. Creighton.

APPENDIX

The drawing of Sheep Ranch City on the following pages is from a fieldman's sketch. Although it was not used in *Calaveras County Illustrated,* the style and date of the drawing seem to confirm that it was done by the same artist who did the sketches for this book. Field sketches were sent to the lithographer's where another artist, using the sketches as a guide, etched the drawings on stone for the final printing process. This procedure obviously permitted the elimination of undesirable details which would be included by a camera. The original of this illustration is owned by George Poore, curator of the Calaveras County Museum in San Andreas.

Poore has been the curator at the museum since it was established in the historic Hall of Records and IOOF building at the old government center on Main Street in San Andreas. During this time the museum has been improved to the point that it is now considered one of the finest in the Mother Lode, if not the entire state.

The museum houses an outstanding Indian basket collection and a pictorial collection which has drawn great interest in recent years.

With the restoration of the Old Courthouse underway as the Bicentennial project for the county it seems certain that this museum complex in San Andreas will take on greater significance in the coming years. The county is also preparing its archives for use by qualified researchers. These archives are thought to be one of the most complete sets of county government records in the state.

In addition to this fine county museum Calaveras County also offers a fine private museum in Murphys under the direction of Dr. R. Coke Wood. The City of Angels museum has some excellent collections and features two fine examples of steam traction engines. Other early vehicles are on display at the Angels Camp facility.

Sheep Ranch City, Calaveras

Sheep Ranch City
Calaveras County, California
Jan. 1885 et.t

County, California, June 1885

INDEX